Finding God

Our Response to God's Gifts

As I open this book, I open myself
to God's presence in my life.
When I allow God's grace to help me,
I see with truth, hear with forgiveness,
and act with kindness.
Thank you God, for your presence in my life.

Barbara F. Campbell, M.Div., D.Min.

James P. Campbell, M.A., D.Min.

LOYOLA PRESS.
A JESUIT MINISTRY
Chicago

Imprimatur	In Conformity
In accordance with c. 827, permission to publish is granted on March 10, 2011 by Rev. Msgr. John F. Canary, Vicar General of the Archdiocese of Chicago. Permission to publish is an official declaration of ecclesiastical authority that the material is free from doctrinal and moral error. No legal responsibility is assumed by the grant of this permission.	The Subcommittee on the Catechism, United States Conference of Catholic Bishops, has found this catechetical text, copyright 2013, to be in conformity with the *Catechism of the Catholic Church*.

Finding God: Our Response to God's Gifts is an expression of the work of Loyola Press, a ministry of the Chicago-Detroit Province of the Society of Jesus.

Senior Consultants
Jane Regan, Ph.D.
Richard Hauser, S.J., Ph.D., S.T.L.
Robert Fabing, S.J., D.Min.

Advisors
Most Reverend Gordon D. Bennett, S.J., D.D.
George A. Aschenbrenner, S.J., S.T.L.
Paul H. Colloton, O.P., D.Min.
Eugene LaVerdiere, S.S.S., Ph.D., S.T.L.
Gerald Darring, M.A.
Thomas J. McGrath, M.A.

Catechetical Staff
Jeanette L. Graham, M.A.
Jean Hopman, O.S.U., M.A.
Joseph Paprocki, D.Min.

Grateful acknowledgment is given to authors, publishers, photographers, museums, and agents for permission to reprint the following copyrighted material; music credits where appropriate can be found at the bottom of each individual song. Every effort has been made to determine copyright owners. In the case of any omissions, the publisher will be pleased to make suitable acknowledgments in future editions. Acknowledgments continue on page 283.

Cover design: Loyola Press
Cover Illustration: Rafael López
Interior design: Loyola Press and Think Bookworks

ISBN-13: 978-0-8294-3173-5
ISBN-10: 0-8294-3173-X

Manufactured in the United States of America.

LOYOLA PRESS.
A JESUIT MINISTRY

3441 N. Ashland Avenue
Chicago, Illinois 60657
(800) 621-1008

www.loyolapress.com
www.ignatianspirituality.com
www.other6.com

Webcrafters, Inc. / Madison, WI, USA / 08-11 / 1st Printing

Contents

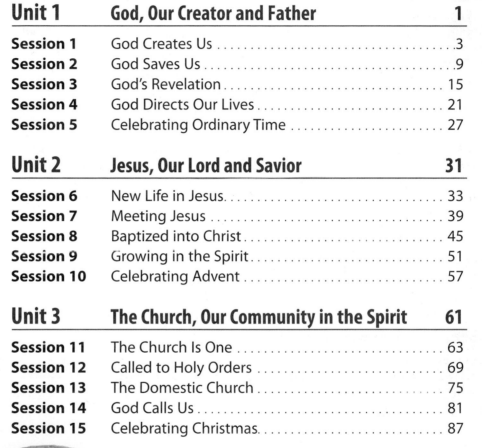

GRADE 5

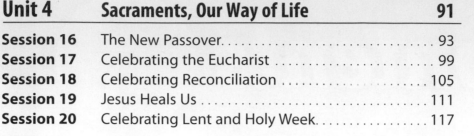

God, Our Creator and Father

Saint Augustine

Saint Augustine is the patron saint of theologians—people who study about God. Augustine wrote a book about his relationship with God. This book is titled *Confessions*.

Saint Augustine

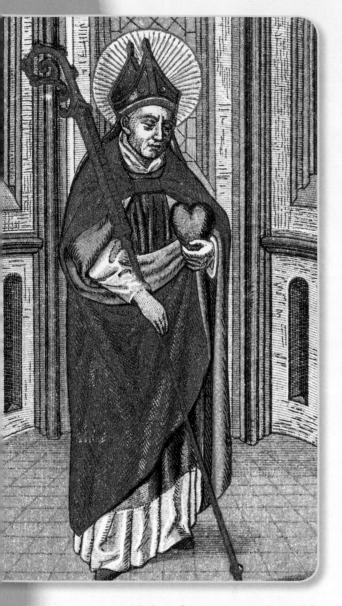

Print of Saint Augustine with a heart, one of his symbols

Although Saint Augustine is a well-known Christian saint, he was not always Christian. He spent his youth getting into trouble with his friends. In *Confessions* Augustine tells us that, as a young boy, he and some of his friends stole pears from a tree. They did not even intend to eat this fruit. In fact they threw it to the pigs. They stole simply for the fun of doing something that was not allowed.

Eventually Augustine became a teacher, but he was not happy with the life he was living. Then he met Ambrose, the bishop of Milan, who led him to study the Bible. While reading the Bible, Augustine realized that he wanted to be close to Jesus Christ.

At the age of 32, Augustine was baptized a Christian. He thought that he would live as a monk. However, the people of the town of Hippo, North Africa (the region where Augustine had been born), wanted him as their leader. So he became bishop of Hippo. As bishop he preached and helped his people. He also wrote about God and religion. He helped Catholics of his time and of every century since then to understand how much God loves them, as Father, Son, and Holy Spirit.

Until his death in A.D. 430, Augustine encouraged his people, telling them to have courage and hope in God. His feast day is August 28.

Think of all the beautiful things that you enjoy through God's gift of life. What things are special to you? Make a list. Share your list with others in your group. Use this as a way to introduce yourself to them.

God Creates Us

Prayer

God, source of all that is, let everything around me speak of you. Help me grow in loving you and trusting in your care.

God Created the World

The Bible tells the story of how God created the earth from what was disorder and chaos. This story of Creation is in the first book of the Bible, Genesis.

> In the beginning, when God created the heavens and the earth, the earth was a formless wasteland, and darkness covered the abyss, while a mighty wind swept over the waters.
>
> *Genesis 1:1–2*

The beginning of Genesis tells how God created the universe and all things in it. The story repeatedly uses the sentence "God saw how good it was."

We, too, experience the wonder and beauty of God's creation when we take time to truly look at the world. By thinking about the world and its beauty and order, we can come to realize that we are part of an order beyond ourselves.

We can come to know God in two ways—from outside and from inside. We can see God's work in the visible world around us, and we can also look inside ourselves and realize that we are incomplete and part of a larger plan.

The sentence, "God saw how good it was," shows God's love for his creation. It also shows the value and dignity of work in God's eyes. Like God's work of creation, our work and efforts are valuable and important too.

Reading God's Word

By faith we understand that the universe was ordered by the word of God.

Hebrews 11:3

Creation Is the Work of the Trinity

All that exists is the work of the Trinity: God as Father, Son, and Holy Spirit.

There is only one God, yet there are Three distinct Persons in God. This is known as the mystery of the Trinity.

Each Person of the Trinity has a special mission.

- ▶ The Father created the world. He made us and everything in the universe.
- ▶ God's Son, Jesus, become man in order to save us.
- ▶ The Holy Spirit gives us grace to believe. The Spirit helps us understand that God is our loving Father and Creator, and that Jesus is the Son of God and our brother.

Prayers Honoring the Trinity

Holy Trinity, Anonymous.

One way we show our belief in the Trinity is by praying the Sign of the Cross. Another way is to pray the Glory Be to the Father. This prayer gives praise to the Three Persons of the Trinity.

A prayer of praise to the Trinity—Father, Son, and Holy Spirit—is called a **doxology**. At mass, the **Eucharistic Prayer** ends with a doxology of praise and adoration of the Trinity.

Link to Liturgy

At Mass our sung expression of praise of the Trinity is the Gloria. With it we proclaim our belief in the Three Persons of the Trinity.

GO TO PAGE 225

God Invites Us to Reflect

Prayer is time we spend with God in our minds and hearts. Often we begin this holy time with the Sign of the Cross.

In the name of the Father, and of the Son, and of the Holy Spirit. Amen.

Imagine yourself in your favorite place. See yourself there. Enjoy being there. What does it look like? What do you hear?

You see Jesus coming to meet you. Greet Jesus. Show him around. Tell him why this place is so special to you.

Walk or sit together. Tell Jesus what's on your mind. He listens, then says something to you. How do you respond? Enjoy each other's company for a while.

Thank Jesus for spending time with you. Thank God for his work of creation. Tell God how glad you are to be able to experience it.

It's time to say good-bye for now. When you are ready, end this prayer time with the Sign of the Cross.

Reflecting on Creation

Think about God and about the beauty and wonders of God's creation.

A. Complete the sentence starters below to tell what things are special to you. Use colored pencils or markers to help you express yourself.

I see …

I hear …

I taste …

I touch …

I smell …

B. What do the beauty and order of creation tell you about God?

_____

_____

C. Write a short prayer to God in thanks and praise of creation.

_____

_____

Living My Faith

Faith Summary

God created the world and continues to love and care for it and for us. There are Three Persons in God, but there is only one God. This mystery is called the Trinity. Each Person in the Trinity has a mission. The Father is the Creator. The Son continues the Father's work in the world. The Holy Spirit helps us know the Father and the Son.

Words I Learned	Ways of Being Like Jesus
doxology	Jesus continues the work of God the Father.
Eucharistic Prayer	*Show respect for the things in creation by recycling your trash at home and around your neighborhood.*

Prayer

Thank you, God, for creating me and caring for me. Thank you for giving me all the people who care for me. Let me show my gratitude by caring for all people and things that you have created.

With My Family

Activity Do something with your family to show your love and respect for the world that God created. Plant flowers, remove weeds, or pick up trash. Use your work to praise God.

Faith on the Go Ask one another: *If you could visit anyplace on earth, where would you go and what would you want to see?*

Family Prayer *Creator God, bless our family. Help us to respect and care for one another and for all the things in creation.*

Think of some problems that exist in the world. Think of some problems that exist in your neighborhood. What problems do you think are important to solve?

God Saves Us

Prayer

Jesus, my Savior, help me find the way to you through the problems I meet. Sometimes it's really tough. Please show me how to do what is right.

The Human Condition

All around us there are reports of war, crime, violence, and unfair treatment of people. There are also stories of heroism and of people being kind to one another. This is the contradictory nature of the **human condition.**

The Bible helps explain the human condition to us. It tells us that we are basically good because God created us to be that way. However, we are part of a human family and have a tendency to sin and to do wrong.

Adam and Eve leaving the Garden of Eden, Amanda Hall.

The Nature of Sin

To explain human weakness, the Book of Genesis in the Bible tells the story of Adam and Eve. They were the parents of the human race. They gave in to temptation and disobeyed God's command. To reject God was their personal decision. Their sin, which resulted in Original Sin, damaged the human family.

Because of Original Sin, we are inclined to do wrong. However, we still have freedom to choose to say yes or no to God. Saying no to God results in personal sin that can lead us to reject God.

What are some ways people say no to God?

_____

_____

_____

Sin and the Promise of Salvation

In one of his letters to the early Christian churches, Saint Paul describes how sin came into the world.

> Therefore, just as through one person sin entered the world, and through sin, death, and thus death came to all.
>
> *Romans 5:12*

Paul is referring to Adam's sin and its devastating effects on all. However, from the beginning, God promised a Savior. The Savior would restore us to friendship with God. This Savior is Jesus, the Son of God, who became man.

Paul describes the promise of Salvation in another of his letters. He makes a contrast: Just as sin and death came into the world through Adam's choice, victory over sin and death comes from Jesus. Jesus reconciles us to God.

Saint Paul wrote his letters, using items such as these.

Meet a Saint

Saint Josephine Bakhita was born in Sudan, in northeastern Africa, in about 1870. At the age of seven, she was stolen by slave traders and sold into slavery. She became the property of an Italian diplomat. In Italy she was sent to a convent school and in 1890 was baptized. Eventually she became a nun. At the convent she did ordinary tasks with a constant smile. She died in 1947 and was declared a saint on October 1, 2000. Her feast day is February 8.

GO TO PAGE 226

Making Good Choices

It is not always easy to do the right thing. You try to do good, but you sometimes fail. You see much good in people, but you also see them act badly, doing such things as fighting or lying. You might even wonder how you can be a better person and still have friends.

Imagine that you are with Jesus when he is speaking to a crowd. You notice his patience and kindness with all the people. You imagine yourself dealing with such a noisy, demanding crowd. Would you be as patient and as kind?

After the crowd leaves, Jesus comes over and sits with you. You tell him that you want to be like him, but sometimes you forget. Ask him to show you how to act when it is confusing or difficult.

Jesus puts his arm around you and invites you to talk to the Father about what's in your heart. You do that quietly. Thank Jesus for showing you how to follow him.

Social Justice Roundtable

We have a responsibility to love one another and treat one another fairly. As you participate in the following roundtable, think about how Jesus loved and cared for those who were treated unfairly.

▶ Read the problem. Brainstorm answers to the question. Then think about what a follower of Jesus would do. Write the group's answers.

▶ Decide on your group's two actions.

▶ Present your final solutions to the other groups.

Problem 1	Someone your age makes a racist remark. *What do you say or do?*
Problem 2	Someone in your class is always bullying other students. *What do you say or do?*
Problem 3	A non-English speaking boy joins your class. Classmates often leave him out and do not include him in their games. *What do you say or do?*
Problem 4	A group of kids makes fun of another student online and posts mean things about her. *What do you say or do?*

Reading God's Word

For since death came through a human being, the resurrection of the dead came also through a human being.

I Corinthians 15:21

Faith Summary

The human family is in a weakened condition, and it is inclined to do wrong because of Original Sin. However, God gave us a Savior, Jesus, who helps us heal our relationship with God.

Words I Learned

human condition

Ways of Being Like Jesus

Jesus showed he loved and cared for people who were poor and sick, or shunned by society. *Comfort those who are excluded from a group or who are being treated unfairly.*

Prayer

Jesus, thank you for being my Savior and bringing me to the Father. Give me the wisdom and courage to know how to help others, particularly those who are being treated unfairly.

With My Family

Activity Think of a community action that your family can perform. You could visit an elderly neighbor, take food to a local food pantry, or collect clothing for a charity. Make a plan and follow through with it together.

Faith on the Go Ask one another: *If you could solve one problem in the world today, what would it be? How would you do it?*

Family Prayer *Loving God, you are so patient with us, even when we struggle. Help us always to be kind and to treat one another fairly.*

God's Revelation

The Bible is divided into the Old Testament and the New Testament. What people can you name from the Old Testament? What stories about them do you know? Share them with the group.

HOLY BIBLE

Prayer

Gracious God, you are faithful to your people through the ages and now. Help me to know that I can always count on you.

The Story of Abraham

Abraham was a just man. He and his wife, Sarah, were elderly, and they didn't have any children. One day God spoke to Abraham and told him to leave his home and to travel to a new land.

Abraham heard and obeyed God's call. He and Sarah trusted in God. At each place the pair stopped in their travels, they set up a shrine to worship God. At one of these stops, God told Abraham about the covenant, or agreement, he wanted to make with him. God said that Abraham would become father of many nations and that Abraham and his wife would have a child.

Abraham accepted the covenant. He promised to worship God as the one true God and to obey him.

adapted from Genesis 15:1–17:22

Abraham, Sarah, and the Angel, Jan Provost, c. 1500.

Abraham and Sarah had a son, who was named Isaac. He in turn had a son called Jacob. They were the ancestors of a people known as the **Hebrews.** Jesus, the Savior that God promised after the fall of Adam and Eve, was also a descendant of Abraham's family.

The story of Salvation on earth begins with Abraham. He is considered a holy person by three of the world's religions: **Judaism,** Christianity, and **Islam.** Judaism, the religion of the Hebrews, or **Jews,** reveres Abraham as its father. Christianity, too, honors him. Islam also recognizes Abraham as an important person.

Reading God's Word

"I am the God of your father," he continued, "the God of Abraham, the God of Isaac, the God of Jacob." *Exodus 3:6*

The Old Testament and the Story of Salvation

Many of the stories in the Old Testament tell about Abraham and his descendants, the Hebrews. The Old Testament recounts the story of Salvation. It reveals God's plan for the human family and the covenant he made with the Hebrew people. The books in the Old Testament are important to Jews, Christians, and **Muslims** (followers of Islam).

The fundamental belief that Christianity received from the Old Testament is that God is One. The principal prayer of Judaism is "Hear, O Israel, the Lord our God is one Lord." Christians believe that the promise of God's covenant was fulfilled in Jesus Christ. They believe the Old Testament is God's **Revelation,** or his communication of himself to us through words and deeds. This Revelation continues in the New Testament.

The Old Testament tells the story of God's people before the time of Jesus. It has 46 books. The New Testament tells the story of Jesus and the early Church. It covers a shorter period of time and has 27 books.

A Jewish boy wears a traditional yarmulke on his head and holds the Torah, a sacred book containing five books from the Old Testament.

Link to Liturgy

The first reading during Sunday Mass is usually from the Old Testament. The second reading is from the New Testament.

GO TO PAGE 227

Living God's Way

Following what God asks of us can be difficult. The Lord's Prayer is a prayer that Jesus taught the disciples. Pray this prayer as the disciples did.

The Lord's Prayer

Our Father, who art in heaven,
hallowed be thy name;
thy kingdom come;
thy will be done on earth as it is in heaven.
Give us this day our daily bread;
and forgive us our trespasses
as we forgive those who trespass against us;
and lead us not into temptation,
but deliver us from evil.
Amen.

Jesus invites you to talk to the Father. Talk to God about his holiness and his will for you. Tell God about your daily needs (your "daily bread"). Thank him for his forgiveness. Talk to him about the temptations you need to avoid. Thank the Father for hearing your prayer.

The Ten Commandments

Review the Ten Commandments at the back of the book. Then find the Ten Commandments in the Bible, Exodus 20:1–17, in which God gives the law to Moses on Mount Sinai.

The Ten Commandments tell you how to live as God wants you to live.

1. Put God first in your life.
2. Do not swear or say God's name in anger.
3. Worship God publicly.
4. Respect your parents and those in authority.
5. Do not hate others or cause them harm.
6. Love and be faithful to your marriage partner.
7. Do not take something that belongs to someone else.
8. Tell the truth.
9. Do not be jealous and want your neighbor's spouse.
10. Do not be jealous when other people have things you want.

Icon of Moses, Livanus Setatou.

Living by the Ten Commandments

List ways you can keep the Ten Commandments.

_____

_____

_____

List things that would break the Ten Commandments.

_____

_____

_____

Living My Faith

Faith Summary

God promised to send a Savior. He made a special Covenant with Abraham and his descendants, who became God's people. God gave us the Ten Commandments. The Old Testament tells the beginning of the story of Salvation, which is fulfilled in Jesus Christ.

Words I Learned

Hebrews Judaism

Islam Muslims

Jews Revelation

Ways of Being Like Jesus

Jesus obeyed God's will as expressed in the Ten Commandments. *Try to honor God above all things. Be kind and compassionate to others.*

Prayer

Loving God, thank you for keeping your promise of sending a Savior and revealing yourself to us in the Bible. Thank you for giving us the Ten Commandments to show us how to be good.

With My Family

Activity By learning the stories of our family history from our parents, our grandparents, and even our great-grandparents, we learn more about ourselves. With members of your family, write a family history.

Faith on the Go Ask one another: *If you could go back in time to be a part of any Old Testament Bible story, which would you choose? Why?*

Family Prayer Pray together the Lord's Prayer. Then spend a few minutes thinking or talking—whichever is more comfortable—about what it means.

God Directs Our Lives

We all depend on one another in many ways. Think of ways that you depend on people like your family, caregivers, teachers, and classmates. Make a list. Then make a second list about how those same people and others depend on you.

Prayer

Creator God, I depend on you for everything, starting with my life. Lead me to gladly search out and follow your will for me, and help me serve your kingdom.

Jesus, the Child, and the Kingdom

Jesus' disciples asked him, "Who is the greatest in the **Kingdom of Heaven**?" He used an example to explain the nature of his kingdom to them—and to us.

Jesus called a child over and told the disciples,

> Amen, I say to you, unless you turn and become like children, you will not enter the kingdom of heaven. Whoever humbles himself like this child is the greatest in the kingdom of heaven. *Matthew 18:3–4*

What do Jesus' words mean? Why did Jesus use the example of a child?

At the time Jesus lived, children counted for almost nothing. They were completely dependent on their families. So in giving a model of a child as having the highest place in his kingdom, Jesus is speaking of someone who is totally dependent and trusting.

Jesus asks the disciples to be humble. This means to recognize our dependence on God and trust in him. Jesus is telling us to let go of our selfish ambitions and trust that God cares for us.

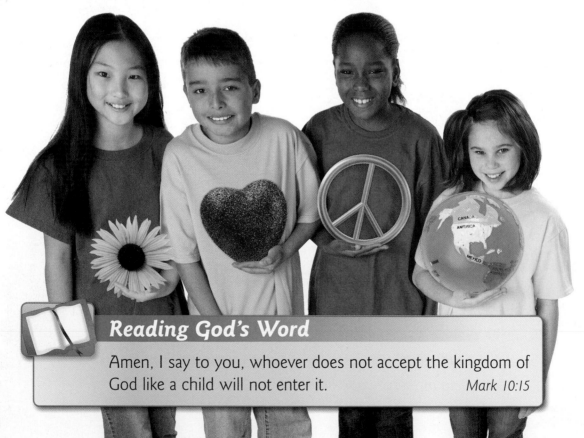

Reading God's Word

Amen, I say to you, whoever does not accept the kingdom of God like a child will not enter it. *Mark 10:15*

The Members of God's Kingdom

Jesus' words tell us what belonging to God's kingdom means. Members of God's kingdom accept God's direction for their lives.

God first revealed that direction in the Old Testament—especially in the Ten Commandments. The Old Testament law is completed in the New Testament. To live the New Law means to practice Christian virtue and live in the grace of the Holy Spirit.

The Son of God became man to proclaim the Kingdom of God. Jesus gave God's direction for us under the New Law in the Beatitudes. They tell us how to share in God's life and be happy. They teach Christian virtue.

How can we grow in virtue? We can study the meaning of the Beatitudes, live out their values, and keep on trying to follow them when it is difficult. Through the Holy Spirit, we receive the grace we need to practice Christian virtue, which the Beatitudes express.

Jesus preaching the Beatitudes, Elizabeth Wang.

When we live the Beatitudes, we are living as members of God's kingdom. We are acting as a sign of God's goodness in the world. We are bringing happiness to others—and to ourselves.

Find the Beatitudes

The Beatitudes are part of Jesus' teaching in the Sermon on the Mount. Read them in Matthew 5:3–12. On a separate sheet of paper, draw a way in which you can live the Beatitudes. Use colored pencils or crayons to illustrate your beatitudes.

GO TO PAGE 228

Asking God for Grace

We can ask God for the grace we need to practice Christian virtue, which the Beatitudes express. When we wake up each day, we can pray the Morning Offering to greet God and to dedicate our day to him.

Morning Offering

My God, I offer you my prayers, works, joys, and sufferings of this day in union with the holy sacrifice of the Mass throughout the world. I offer them for all the intentions of your Son's Sacred Heart, for the salvation of souls, reparation for sin, and the reunion of Christians.
Amen.

After you pray the Morning Offering, spend some time with God. Tell God what you will be doing for the rest of the day. Ask for his help and blessing on yourself and on all you meet.

The Meaning of the Beatitudes

In this session you learned about the Beatitudes. Read the Beatitudes at the back of the book. Write the beatitude that goes with each statement below.

1. We feel sad when we see people in bad situations.

   Blessed are they who mourn, for they will be comfortable.

2. We work to end bad feelings and arguments.

   Bless are peacemakers for they will be called children of god

3. Our possessions are not the most important things in our lives.

   Bless are poor in spirt for their is a kingdom of heaven

4. We do not get angry easily, and we are kind and gentle with others.

   Bless are they who are persucuted

5. We do our best to see that everyone is treated fairly.

6. We forgive those who hurt us.

7. We do something good even when others laugh at us.

8. We are loyal to God's commands and act with good intentions.

Living My Faith

Faith Summary

Jesus taught us how to serve God's kingdom. We are called to be dependent on God and trust in him. Jesus gave us the Beatitudes to show how to share God's life fully and be happy.

Christ Our Brother,
Brother Michael Moran, C.P.

Words I Learned

Kingdom of Heaven

Ways of Being Like Jesus

Jesus was humble and recognized that we depend on God for all things. *Show concern for others by volunteering to help those who are less fortunate.*

Prayer

Thank you, Jesus, for giving me the Beatitudes to show me how to live. Help me live them in my life every day.

With My Family

Activity Think of ways your family can live out the Beatitudes. List ideas for each one. Post the list on your refrigerator and try to check off at least one each week.

Faith on the Go Ask one another: *If you were in the crowd listening to Jesus give the Sermon on the Mount, what is one question you would have asked him?*

Family Prayer Loving God, let us be like little children and depend completely upon you. Help us to see the needs of others and care for them as you care for us.

Celebrating Ordinary Time

The liturgical year commemorates the life of Jesus, starting with the preparation for his coming and his birth, his Death and Resurrection, to his Ascension, and his sending the Holy Spirit upon the apostles at Pentecost. Every day of the year is holy because God is always present to us.

During the season of Ordinary Time, we celebrate our call to follow Jesus every day. We celebrate Ordinary Time in two parts. The first part follows the Christmas season and continues until Ash Wednesday. The second part follows the Easter season and goes through late fall. Toward the end of Ordinary Time, the Church celebrates All Saints Day and All Souls Day.

Ordinary Time does not refer to "common time," but rather it means "counted time." It comes from the word *ordinal* and refers to time in a certain order.

Prayer

Dear Jesus, be with me each day of Ordinary Time. I know you love me and guide my steps every day.

We Grow with the Sacraments During Ordinary Time

Ordinary Time is a time to grow in our faith. We can use this time to try to live the way Jesus wants us to live by focusing on our celebration of the seven **sacraments**—Baptism, Confirmation, the Eucharist, Penance and Reconciliation, Anointing of the Sick, Holy Orders, and Matrimony. When we celebrate a sacrament, we experience the grace of God.

▶ What are some ways that you can grow and live like Jesus?

▶ What are some ways that you can grow by celebrating the sacraments?

▶ What are some ways that you can grow and serve others?

How Can I Grow?

During Ordinary Time we grow closer to God through the celebration of the sacraments. Draw a picture representing one of the sacraments and write a sentence explaining its importance to you.

Reading God's Word

The LORD, your God, you shall worship; then I will bless your food and drink.

Exodus 23:25

Mass During Ordinary Time

When you go to Mass during Ordinary Time, you will hear readings about Jesus' life and his teachings. These readings remind us how Jesus lived and treated others so that we can try to live like him. Sacramentals are sacred signs instituted by the Church which help us grow in the grace we receive in the sacraments. We can see, hear, touch, and use sacramentals every day to connect our lives with Jesus.

Sixth station of the cross, Laura James.

What We Experience

As you enter your church, you will bless yourself with holy water. On the walls of the church, you will see the Stations of the Cross. These are two more examples of sacramentals. Blessing ourselves and praying the Stations of the Cross help us prepare to receive the grace of God.

God Touches My Life

Think of your life during Ordinary Time this last year. How has God touched your life? Was it through an experience at church? Was it through an everyday event at home or at school? Complete the sentence below to share your ideas.

During Ordinary Time, God touched my life when _____

_____.

? Did You Know?

The liturgical color for Ordinary Time is green.

GO TO PAGE 229

Living My Faith

Faith Summary

Ordinary Time is the part of the Church calendar that falls outside of the four liturgical seasons during which we celebrate the mystery of Christ in very special and particular ways. We use this time to help us grow by participating regularly in the celebration of the sacraments and using sacramentals so that we can live the way Jesus wants us to live.

Word I Learned

sacraments

Ways of Being Like Jesus

Jesus loved to spend time with children. *Always have a smile and a kind word to say to younger children who look up to you.*

Prayer

Dear God, thank you for the opportunity to grow in my faith during Ordinary Time. Help me to hear and follow your words in my daily life.

With My Family

Activity When you go to church during Ordinary Time, look for examples of the sacramentals described in this session. Talk about what you see.

Faith on the Go Ask one another: *Why are the sacraments so important?*

Family Prayer Use Ordinary Time to invite family members to grow by praying at bedtime for someone who did a kindness for them that day.

Jesus, Our Lord and Savior

UNIT 2

Saint Alphonsus Liguori

Saint Alphonsus Liguori was a Doctor of the Church, influential for his writings. He wrote about making good moral choices and about ways to pray.

31

Saint Alphonsus Liguori

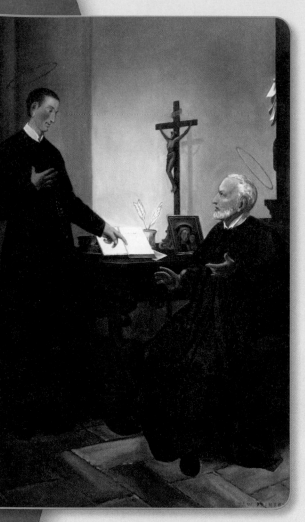

Saint Alphonsus (right) with Saint Gerard Majella, J. W. Printon C.S.S.R.

Alphonsus Liguori was born into a noble Italian family in 1696. He was a brilliant student and received a degree in law at the age of only 16. For 11 years Alphonsus was a famous lawyer but grew very disturbed by the corruption he saw in the courts. He prayed to know God's will. Finally at Scala, in Italy, he had a vision of his vocation and decided to become a priest.

Despite many difficulties, he founded an order of priests and brothers called the Redemptorists, whose goal was to preach and teach in the rural areas and city slums. He became a bishop known for preaching and bringing people back to God. At the end of his life, Alphonsus had many physical sufferings and went through a period of spiritual discouragement, but he did not turn from God. He died in 1787 and was canonized in 1839. His feast day is August 1.

Alphonsus taught people to pray by imagining themselves with Jesus in the Gospels and talking to him openly. He taught people to open their hearts to Jesus. He also encouraged people to pray often before the Blessed Sacrament.

Alphonsus's personal outpouring of love for Jesus was expressed in hymns. One of these is still a popular Italian Christmas song: "You Come Down from the Stars." In 1871 Alphonsus was declared a Doctor of the Church.

Handwriting of Saint Alphonsus

What is happening in this picture? Jesus teaches us that praying with our family can help us strengthen our faith.

New Life in Jesus

Prayer

Jesus, you lived your life the way God our Father wanted. Help me to do the same thing with my life.

Jesus' Mission on Earth

The Son of God became man to fulfill a mission. With Adam's sin, there was a break in the relationship between God and humanity. The Son of God came to heal that relationship. God becoming man while remaining divine is a **mystery** that we call the **Incarnation.** A mystery is something we believe although we do not completely understand it.

Through his life, Death, and Resurrection, Jesus reconciles humanity to God. This is the reason Jesus lived on earth. In fact the name *Jesus* means "God saves."

Jesus is both divine and human, true God and true man. As divine, Jesus is our Lord and Savior and speaks for God. As human, Jesus speaks for us. He knows our needs as well as our ability to love.

Icon of Jesus as the Good Shepherd.

Jesus' Church Continues His Mission

Jesus' mission on earth continues for all time. Through the Holy Spirit, Jesus established a Church to carry on his mission.

The Church passes on the principles of faith taught by the apostles, Jesus' followers. It has carried on this role for centuries. The Church also speaks to the needs of the present time. As the sign and symbol of God's presence in the world, the Church is called to address all that concerns God; which includes working for justice and for peace.

The Role of the Holy Spirit in Jesus' Mission

It is with the help of the Holy Spirit that the Church carries on the teachings of Jesus and continues his mission on earth.

The Spirit also works through individuals. In Baptism and Confirmation, the Spirit gives us the help we need to fulfill our mission to be living signs of Jesus on earth. We call this help **sanctifying grace.** This special grace is a gift from God that we cannot earn through our own efforts.

Meet a Holy Person

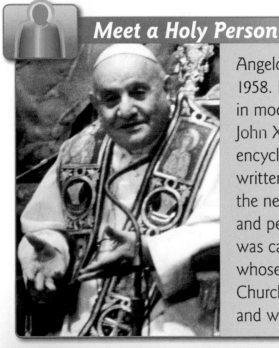

Angelo Roncalli was elected pope in 1958. His papacy was a turning point in modern Church history. As Pope John XXIII, Roncalli wrote important encyclicals—pastoral letters that are written by the pope—that emphasized the need to work for economic justice and peace. His greatest achievement was calling the Second Vatican Council, whose purpose was to renew the Church. Blessed John XXIII died in 1963 and was beatified in 2000.

GO TO PAGE 230

The Incarnation

Jesus has called you to be a member of his Church, to live as a sign of Jesus' presence on earth.

Show your belief and faith in Jesus and his teachings by praying the Apostles' Creed silently as you listen to it prayed aloud.

Apostles' Creed

I believe in God,
the Father almighty,
Creator of heaven and earth,
and in Jesus Christ, his only Son, our Lord,
who was conceived by the Holy Spirit,
born of the Virgin Mary,
suffered under Pontius Pilate,
was crucified, died and was buried;
he descended into hell;
on the third day he rose again from the dead;
he ascended into heaven,
and is seated at the right hand of God the Father almighty;
from there he will come to judge the living and the dead.

I believe in the Holy Spirit,
the holy catholic Church,
the communion of saints,
the forgiveness of sins,
the resurrection of the body,
and life everlasting. Amen.

Spend a few minutes with Jesus. Tell him in your own words how much you believe and trust in him.

The Apostles' Creed

From its very beginning—from the time of the apostles—the Church has taught people about God's plan. The basic teachings of the Church are in the Apostles' Creed. The Apostles' Creed summarizes our beliefs as Christians.

What Does the Apostles' Creed Say?

Review the Apostles' Creed. Then read each statement about the Creed. Write **T** for true or **F** for false.

1. _____ It recognizes that there are three Persons in one God.

2. _____ It describes the Father as Creator.

3. _____ It talks about Adam and Eve.

4. _____ It refers to the mystery of the Incarnation.

5. _____ It mentions that the Bible is the Word of God.

6. _____ Jesus' work of Salvation is summarized.

7. _____ The Last Supper is described.

8. _____ It says Jesus returned to the Father after his life on earth.

9. _____ The role of the pope is explained.

10. _____ It mentions that after death there is resurrection.

Link to Liturgy

The word *creed* comes from the Latin word *credo*, which means "I believe." The creed we pray at Mass is called the Nicene Creed. It gets its name from Nicea, an ancient city in what is now Turkey, where the first Church council was held in A.D. 325.

Jesus with the apostles

Living My Faith

Faith Summary

We call the mystery of God becoming man in Jesus the Incarnation. Jesus' mission on earth continues through his Church. As members of the Church, we are signs of Jesus' presence on earth. God, through the Holy Spirit, gives us sanctifying grace, which helps us live like Jesus.

Words I Learned	Ways of Being Like Jesus
Incarnation **mystery** **sanctifying grace**	Jesus followed the practices of Judaism during his life, actively participating in holy days and following traditions. *Be an active participant in your parish by volunteering to be a server at Mass.*

Prayer

Jesus, thank you for loving and caring for us so much that you became one of us to save us. Thank you for making me a living sign of God's presence in the world.

With My Family

Activity Take a ride to two or three churches near you, or visit the Web sites of Catholic churches around the country. Look at their bulletins and compare how these churches are trying to live out Jesus' mission.

Faith on the Go Ask one another: *If Jesus joined us for dinner tonight, what one question would you ask him?*

Family Prayer *Dear God, thank you for blessing us with your Son, Jesus. Through him we are saved. Help us to remember your love and to love one another.*

We sometimes use special gestures to make contact with other people. The gestures show that we are connected. Gestures are defined by the culture or group using them. What are some gestures you use with your family or your friends?

Meeting Jesus

Prayer

Jesus, help me recognize the many ways you are present in the world and how you touch my life every day. Let me pass on your love and goodness to the people I meet.

The Seven Sacraments

Jesus Christ touches our lives when we receive the sacraments. Each sacrament is associated with signs: objects, words, and actions. Each sign brings God's grace and blessings in a special way.

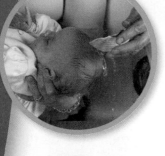

Baptism

In Baptism we receive new life in Christ. Baptism takes away Original Sin and gives us a new birth in the Holy Spirit. Its signs are water, oil, a candle, and a white garment.

Confirmation

In Confirmation the Holy Spirit strengthens our life of faith. Its signs are laying hands on a person's head (most often by a bishop) and anointing with **Chrism,** oil mixed with perfume. Like Baptism, Confirmation is celebrated only once.

Eucharist

The Eucharist nourishes our life of faith. Its signs are the bread and wine we receive—the Body and Blood of Christ.

Link to Liturgy

New adult members of the Church are traditionally welcomed during the Easter Vigil service. Unbaptized adults receive Baptism, Confirmation, and the Eucharist at that time. The entire process of becoming a new Church member is called the Rite of Christian Initiation of Adults (RCIA).

Penance and Reconciliation

In the Sacrament of Penance and Reconciliation, we celebrate God's forgiveness. Forgiveness requires being sorry for our sins. In this sacrament Jesus' healing grace is received through absolution by a priest.

Anointing of the Sick

This sacrament unites a sick person's sufferings with those of Jesus and brings healing and forgiveness of sins. A person is anointed with the oil of the sick and receives the laying on of hands from a priest.

Holy Orders

In Holy Orders, men are ordained as priests to be leaders of the community, as bishops to shepherd the Church, or as permanent deacons to serve the community. The sacrament involves the laying on of hands for all three, and the anointing with Chrism for bishops and priests.

Matrimony

In Matrimony a baptized man and woman are united with each other as a sign of unity between Jesus and his Church. Matrimony requires the consent of the couple, as expressed in the marriage promises.

GO TO PAGE 231

Prayer of Gratitude

In the Gospel of Mark, Chapter 5, we read the story of Jesus' raising Jairus's daughter.

Imagine you are one of the people present in the crowd when Jairus arrives to talk to Jesus. Jairus really believes that Jesus can help. And he's right.

Jesus touches the girl. She awakens and gets up. Jesus tells the parents to get her something to eat. Jesus really cares for her.

He cares for you too. In what ways do you need Jesus' care? In your heart ask Jesus for what you need.

Listen for his answer. Thank him for his love.

We Are Blessed

In the sacraments we recognize that God the Father is the source of all blessings. The sacraments are blessings we receive from God in his generosity and unshakable love. Jesus is the Father's greatest blessing to us. Through the Holy Spirit, we become adopted children of God.

Find Your Blessings

We are constantly receiving blessings from God. The help and blessings we give one another reflect this. Write about one special blessing you have received from someone. Tell why it is important to you.

_____

_____

_____

_____

As followers of Jesus, we are called to be a blessing to others. Write about one way you have blessed someone else. Tell how your blessing made a difference in that person's life.

_____

_____

_____

_____

Faith Summary

Jesus' touch healed people and brought them life and peace. The sacraments celebrate Jesus' presence among us today. A sacrament is a sign by which Jesus shares God's life and blessings—his grace—with us.

Jesus raising Jairus's daughter

Word I Learned

Chrism

Ways of Being Like Jesus

Jesus brings healing and peace to others. *Give words of comfort to those who are sick and help with their needs.*

Prayer

Jesus, thank you for the sacraments so that I can experience your presence in my life and receive your blessings.

With My Family

Activity Gather in a circle and have each person say one blessing he or she feels that day. Go around the circle until each person calls out a blessing, without repeating.

Faith on the Go Ask one another: *If you could bless one person with any gift you wanted, whom would you choose, and what would you give?*

Family Prayer Father, our family is blessed with so many gifts. Thank you for your loving friendship. Help us stay close to you through the sacraments.

How do you become part of a group? What ceremonies do you go through when you join? What are the duties and responsibilities of members of a group? Think about all the groups you belong to and what it means to be a member.

Baptized into Christ

Prayer

Jesus, through Baptism, you made me part of your community, the Church. Help me show through my actions that I am learning to accept my responsibilities as a member of your Church.

The Sacrament of Baptism

Baptism is a call to a new birth and life—life in the Holy Spirit. Baptism unites us with the Death and Resurrection of Jesus, is necessary for Salvation, and welcomes us into the Church.

The Rite of Baptism

Water is the main sign of Baptism. While water is necessary for human life, it can also destroy, as with floods. In nature, water can be a sign of both life and death. It is appropriate then that water is the sign used to show our dying and rising with Jesus.

In the celebration of Baptism, a person is immersed in water. He or she goes all the way into the water and then comes out. This action is a symbol of dying to sin and rising to a new life in Christ. Sometimes water is poured over a person's head. The celebrant calls on the Trinity: "I baptize you in the name of the Father, and of the Son, and of the Holy Spirit."

The person being baptized puts on a white garment. It symbolizes that the person is a new creation, now clothed in Christ.

A child being baptized is anointed with two oils: the **oil of catechumens** is put on the chest, and Chrism is put on the top of the head. These special oils are blessed by the bishop and symbolize strength and healing.

Oil of catechumens

Link to Liturgy

The Paschal Candle is lit during the celebration of Baptism. When an infant is baptized, the family receives a candle lit from the Paschal Candle. This light is entrusted to them so that they may help keep the light of faith burning brightly in the life of the child.

The Effects of Baptism

Through Baptism a person receives forgiveness from Original Sin as well as personal sins. The baptized person receives sanctifying grace. Baptism seals the person with a permanent spiritual mark. That is why the sacrament can be celebrated only once.

Peaceful Server, Regina Kubelka.

What Baptism Calls Us to Do

Baptism makes us members of the Church, whose mission we share.

One of our duties as members is **stewardship.** Stewardship calls Catholics to share their time, money and goods, and talents to contribute to God's kingdom on earth.

How Are You a Steward?

You can practice stewardship by giving service to the Church. List some ways that people of your age give service to the Church.

_____

_____

_____

List two ways that you can use your talents to serve the Church.

_____

_____

? Did You Know?

Catechumens are people learning about the Christian life and preparing to live as Christians. Signed with the cross, they have a special relationship with the Church.

GO TO PAGE 232

Being a Child of Light

One of the signs of Baptism is a lit candle. It shows our responsibility to keep the flame of faith burning and to be the living signs of Jesus on earth.

Pause and think about the symbol of the lit candle. See it in your mind.

Your parents received a lit candle at your Baptism. These are some of the words they heard when they were given the candle: "You have been enlightened by Christ. Walk always as children of light and keep the flame of faith alive in your heart."

Think about these words. Which of them have special meaning for you today?

Ask Jesus to help you walk as a child of light.

We Are a Light for the World

The candle you received at your Baptism was lit from the Easter Candle, also known as the Paschal Candle. Its flame represents Jesus Christ, The Light of the World. When you received the candle, you received this light too. Jesus lights your way to God. Now you must help light the way for others.

Paschal Candle, Julie Lonneman.

Be a Light in the World

A. Work with a small group to make a list of ways that Jesus lights our way to God.

_____

_____

_____

_____

B. Make a list of ways that you can be a light for others.

_____

_____

_____

_____

C. Write your own personal promise that helps you live as a baptized member of the Church.

I promise to be a light in the world by _____

_____

_____

Living My Faith

Faith Summary

Baptism is a call to new life in Jesus Christ through the Holy Spirit. Baptism unites us with the Death and Resurrection of Jesus and welcomes us into the Church. Baptism makes us children of the Father, members of the Church, and Temples of the Holy Spirit.

Words I Learned

oil of catechumens
stewardship

Ways of Being Like Jesus

Jesus accomplished his mission on earth. He devoted himself entirely to teaching about God and his kingdom. *Offer your talents and give service to the Church and the community to share in Jesus' mission.*

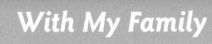

Prayer

Loving God, thank you for welcoming me into your community, the Church, through Baptism.

With My Family

Activity Talk with your family about your Baptism. Try to find some pictures or videos of the celebration. If you still have your baptismal candle, you might light it while you do this.

Faith on the Go Ask one another: *If I could be part of any ministry in our Church, what would it be? Why?*

Family Prayer Dear God, thank you for the Church, our faith family. Help us live our baptismal promises and be active members in your kingdom on earth.

As you grow up, you have more and more responsibilities as a member of your family and your community. What responsibilities and duties do you have now that you didn't have a year ago? What responsibilities will you get when you're older?

Growing in the Spirit

Prayer

Jesus, teach me what it means to be holy. May your Holy Spirit, whom I received at my Baptism, help me be strong in my faith.

Our Mission as Christians

Just as the apostles were given a mission, all Christians have a special mission, a call to **holiness.** This means living a life dedicated to God and to the mission of the Church to proclaim the good news of Salvation offered through Jesus Christ.

Just as the Holy Spirit helped the apostles fulfill their mission, the Spirit acts in our lives and calls us to continue the mission of Jesus.

Confirmation and Our Mission

We can lead holy lives only with the help of God's grace, which we receive in the sacraments. We first received sanctifying grace in Baptism. Through that sacrament our sins were forgiven, and we received the help we need to live for God and others. Confirmation continues and completes Baptism. In Confirmation, as in Baptism, we receive sanctifying grace.

Through Confirmation our relationship with God is strengthened. We ask God to send us the Holy Spirit, the **Advocate,** or Helper, to give us the **Gifts of the Holy Spirit.** These gifts are a permanent willingness that makes it possible for us to do what God asks of us. The gifts are **wisdom, understanding, counsel, fortitude, knowledge, piety,** and **fear of the Lord.** In Confirmation our bond with Jesus is made stronger so that we can better witness to Christ. We are witnesses to Christ when our actions reflect Jesus' presence in the world and show our faith in God.

Did You Know?

Different countries have observed various customs at Pentecost, the feast at which we celebrate the Holy Spirit descending upon the apostles. In Italy, rose petals, symbolic of fiery tongues, were scattered from the ceilings of churches. In France trumpets were blown during Mass to recall the sound of the strong, driving wind that accompanied the arrival of the Holy Spirit.

The Sacrament of Confirmation

Confirmation is a Sacrament of Initiation in which baptized Christians receive help from the Holy Spirit to fulfill their mission.

Who Can Be Confirmed

The person being confirmed

- ▶ has reached the age of reason, which is defined as about the age of seven.
- ▶ professes the faith and wants to receive the sacrament.
- ▶ is in the state of grace, a state of friendship with God.
- ▶ is ready to live as a witness to Christ.

As in Baptism, a person can celebrate Confirmation only once.

The Rite and Signs of Confirmation

A bishop is the usual celebrant of the Sacrament of Confirmation. When administering the sacrament, the bishop first extends his hands over those to be confirmed and calls on God: "Send your Holy Spirit upon them to be their helper and guide."

At this point each person being confirmed is anointed with Chrism. Then the bishop makes the Sign of the Cross on the forehead of the person as he says "Be sealed with the Gift of the Holy Spirit."

The Effects of Confirmation

Confirmation gives sanctifying grace. We deepen our life in the Holy Spirit and form a closer bond with Jesus. The Holy Spirit helps us believe, pray, love, and perform good acts.

GO TO PAGE 233

Help from the Holy Spirit

The Holy Spirit guides you in your life. The Spirit helps you in your call as a Christian to live a holy life and be a sign of the living presence of Jesus on earth.

Prayer to the Holy Spirit

Come, Holy Spirit, fill the hearts of your faithful.
And kindle in them the fire of your love.
Send forth your Spirit and they shall be created.
And you will renew the face of the earth.
Let us pray.

Lord,
by the light of the Holy Spirit
you have taught the hearts of your faithful.
In the same Spirit
help us to relish what is right
and always rejoice in your consolation.
We ask this through Christ our Lord.
Amen.

Understanding the Sacraments

Confirmation Is a Call

Baptism makes you a part of the Church. Confirmation calls you to take on more responsibility as a Church member. Through this sacrament you are called to show Jesus' presence by participating more fully in the mission of the Church and by working for justice and peace.

Complete the chart about Baptism and Confirmation.

	Baptism	Confirmation
Grace received		
Signs during the rite		
Number of times received		
What it calls us to do		

Reading God's Word

The wind blows where it wills, and you can hear the sound it makes, but you do not know where it comes from or where it goes; so it is with everyone who is born of the Spirit.

John 3:8

Faith Summary

In Confirmation we are sealed with the Holy Spirit, and we receive the strength we need to give witness to the faith. Confirmation completes Baptism. Through the Spirit we receive the grace to fulfill our call as Christians, to live holy lives, and to participate in the Church's mission.

Words I Learned

Advocate	Gifts of the Holy Spirit	understanding
counsel	holiness	wisdom
fear of the Lord	knowledge	
fortitude	piety	

Ways of Being Like Jesus

During his life Jesus prayed to the Father, comforted and healed others, and forgave those who hurt him. *Forgive those who hurt you and pray for those who cannot forgive.*

Prayer

Dear Holy Spirit, thank you for being the Lord and Giver of Life. Thank you for giving me the strength to be a living sign of Jesus' presence in the world.

With My Family

Activity Talk with your parents and other family members about their Confirmation. Ask if they picked new names for Confirmation and if so, how they chose their names.

Faith on the Go Ask one another: *When have you felt the presence of the Holy Spirit in your life?*

Family Prayer *Holy Spirit, come into our lives. Strengthen and guide us while helping us to spread the flame of faith to others that we meet.*

Celebrating Advent

Advent is the season of the Church's liturgical year in which we prepare for the coming of Jesus. During Advent we look into our hearts and ask ourselves if we are living the life Jesus has called us to live. We ask God to be with us as we prepare to celebrate Jesus coming into the world.

The first Sunday of Advent marks the beginning of the liturgical year. During Advent we also celebrate the Feast of the Immaculate Conception on December 8. Advent, which has four Sundays, ends on Christmas Eve.

The word *Advent* comes from the Latin word *adventus*, which means "arrival" or "coming." Advent is a season of grace during which we pray that we may be ready to welcome Jesus into our hearts and our homes.

Prayer

Jesus, help us to use this time of Advent to ready ourselves for the celebration of your birth. Be with us as we prepare our hearts and homes to welcome you into the world.

We Prepare During Advent

Advent is a time to prepare our hearts, our homes, and our churches for the coming of Jesus. We can prepare by celebrating the Sacraments of the Eucharist and of Reconciliation. The Eucharist gives us the strength to live as God asks us. Reconciliation is a way to show that we want to make better choices.

Write one way you can prepare for Jesus for each week of Advent. Ask yourself "What can I do to help prepare the way for Jesus?"

Week 1 _____

Week 2 _____

Week 3 _____

Week 4 _____

God's Gift of Eternal Life

God gave us the gift of Jesus so that we may have eternal life through Jesus Christ, our Lord. Think about this gift. Close your eyes and imagine God walking beside you. What are you saying to him? Do you thank him for the gift of Jesus? Open your eyes. Now write your thoughts in a letter to God.

_____

_____

_____

_____

_____

Reading God's Word

. . . Go and prosper: the LORD is favorable to the undertaking you are engaged in.

Judges 18:6

Mass During Advent

When you go to Mass during Advent, you will hear readings about God's promise to send a Savior. Readings will include the message of the prophets and of John the Baptist, calling people to prepare for the birth of Jesus. Think about how we as God's people today also need to prepare to fully accept Jesus, God's gift of eternal life.

What We Experience

When you walk into your church during Advent, look for the **baptismal font.** This is where new Christians are welcomed into the Church. It was through our own Baptism that we became children of God. Can you locate the Reconciliation room? It is through Reconciliation that we receive God's forgiveness. Celebrating this sacrament during Advent allows us to prepare our hearts for Jesus. Next, look at the altar, where the priest consecrates the bread and wine, transforming them into the Body and Blood of Christ. God shares his grace with us through the sacraments. Each sacrament was instituted by Christ and given to the Church so that we can receive the grace we need to live holy lives.

The Gift of the Sacraments

The sacraments are God's gift to us. In the box, draw a symbol of one of the sacraments you read about in this session.

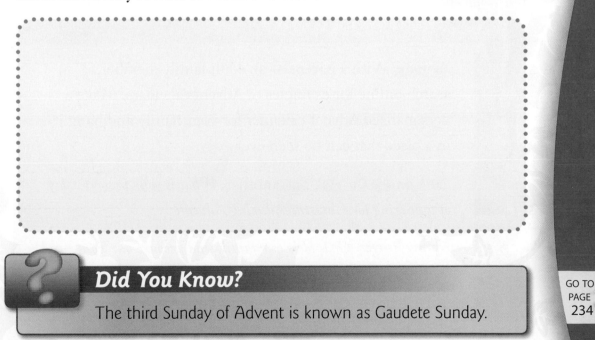

Did You Know?

The third Sunday of Advent is known as Gaudete Sunday.

GO TO PAGE 234

Faith Summary

The first Sunday of Advent is the beginning of the liturgical year. During Advent we can celebrate the Sacrament of Reconciliation to help us prepare to welcome Jesus. We thank God for giving us Jesus, a gift that allows us to have eternal life.

Words I Learned

baptismal font

Ways of Being Like Jesus

Jesus cared for Mary and Joseph. *Tell family members how much you love them.*

Prayer

Dear God, thank you for giving us an opportunity to prepare to celebrate the birth of your Son. I know that as I prepare to welcome Jesus, you are here to guide my words and choices.

With My Family

Activity With a parent or an adult family member, search online for examples of Advent calendars. Make a personalized Advent calender for your family and hang it in a place that can be seen every day.

Faith on the Go Ask one another: *What is your favorite way of preparing for Christmas during Advent?*

Family Prayer God, bless our family and prepare our home and hearts to welcome your Son, Jesus Christ, into the world.

The Church, Our Community in the Spirit

Saint Ignatius of Loyola

Saint Ignatius of Loyola was the founder of an order of priests and brothers called the Jesuits. Their mission is to serve the Church.

Saint Ignatius of Loyola

Ignatius of Loyola, born in 1491 in Spain, started his career as a soldier in service to his king. Because of a wound to his leg, he had to spend months in bed. While recovering he had only two books to read. One was about Jesus, and the other was about the saints. Studying them changed his life. Ignatius decided to devote himself to serving God by imitating Jesus.

During a time of spiritual growth, Ignatius developed a plan of meditation called the *Spiritual Exercises*. This work aims to help people discover God's will for them and to give them the courage to follow God's call. The *Exercises* first guide people through meditations on sinfulness and living the Ten Commandments. Then people are asked to imagine themselves in the Gospel and follow along with Jesus' life, Death, and Resurrection. The goal of the Gospel is to lead people to a life of generous service, prompted by a love of Jesus Christ and the desire to follow him.

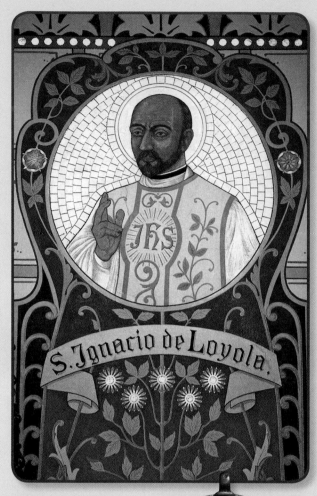

Spanish painting and medal with Jesuit logo

Ignatius's vision and ideas attracted a band of followers, and he eventually founded a community of priests and brothers called the Society of Jesus. Its members are called the Jesuits. Since Ignatius's time, Jesuits have been dedicated to serving the Church community by establishing schools and sending members throughout the world to spread the Good News about Jesus. Saint Ignatius's feast day is July 31.

View of Pamplona, where Ignatius was wounded

How does your family celebrate Christmas? How do you celebrate Easter? What do you know about different ways to celebrate Church holidays around the world? Share your information with others.

The Church Is One

Prayer

Jesus, help me see that I am a brother or sister of all people you have called. Help me accept and appreciate all the members of your Church.

Different Roles for Church Members

All baptized people are part of the community of believers. The members of the Church are called to be holy and answer God's call in many ways.

▶ The pope, bishops, priests, and deacons receive the Sacrament of Holy Orders and form the **clergy.** Bishops and priests form the **priesthood.**

▶ Some people answer the call to lead a **religious life,** following Jesus by living in a community and embracing its practices. They make promises called **vows.** Through the vows of poverty, chastity, and obedience, they promise to live simply, to live in a chaste manner, and to obey those in authority.

▶ Members of the Church who are not priests or in religious life make up the **laity.** The laity are called to be witnesses to Christ in the world and to foster gospel values in society.

Unity in Beliefs

The Church keeps its unity by being faithful to the teachings of the apostles. Review the Apostles' Creed on page 36. Begin with the words "I believe in the Holy Spirit." Then match each phrase below with its meaning.

1. _____ the holy catholic Church

2. _____ communion of saints

3. _____ forgiveness of sins

4. _____ resurrection of the body

a. God gives us pardon.

b. We will share new life in Christ after death.

c. The Church is for all.

d. All the holy—living and dead—are united.

Reading God's Word

There is neither Jew nor Greek, there is neither slave nor free person, there is not male and female; for you are all one in Christ Jesus.

Galatians 3:28

The Pope's Role in the Church's Unity

A visible sign of the unity in the Church is the pope, together with the bishops who administer local dioceses. The pope and bishops receive their authority as successors of the apostles. They ensure fidelity to the apostles' teachings. The pope is the successor of Saint Peter, whom Jesus chose as the leader of the Church. As such the pope has full authority over the Church.

Pope Benedict XVI

The Servant of the Servants of God

Gregory the Great (540–604) was a pope who devoted himself to pastoral work. Living at a time of political disorder, he took on the task of providing for people's needs.

Gregory promoted devotion to the Stations of the Cross, a way to reflect upon and retrace Jesus' steps on the way to his crucifixion. Gregory also reformed the liturgy and added the Lord's Prayer to the Mass. In addition the religious music known as Gregorian chant was named for him. He was a noted writer who gave practical advice to help bishops and leaders serve their communities. Gregory was also interested in **evangelization**, or spreading the news about Jesus.

Gregory called himself the "servant of the servants of God," a title that popes still use. Indeed, his words and actions became an example for later popes to follow.

Gregory the Great and Vatican City

GO TO PAGE 235

The Apostles' Creed

Recall the Apostles' Creed on page 36. The Apostles' Creed is the prayer of faith.

When you pray the Creed, think about each line as you pray it. Think particularly about the meaning of these lines: "I believe in the Holy Spirit, the holy catholic Church, the communion of saints."

Think about all the people you know in your parish. Think about how we are all brothers and sisters in Christ despite our differences in age, places of birth, talents, and interests.

Jesus, we are all people living your word through the Church. We all believe in your Eternal Word and the goodness of your mission. Thank you for bringing us together so that we may pray and live as a community of believers. Amen.

Spend some time talking with Jesus in personal reflection and thank him for always being with you.

Examining the Eastern Tradition

Icon, *Christ of the Sinai,*
Dr. Elizabeth Hudgins.

While the Church is united as a community of believers, different traditions were a part of the Church from its beginning. These differences were the result of the division of the Roman Empire into the West and the East. While we are one Church, there are some differences in our traditions and how we experience the liturgy.

Churches that follow the Eastern tradition have a screen across the front of the altar. Gates in the screen are opened at the start of the liturgy. The priest stays mostly behind the gate with his back to the congregation. A choir and the congregation sing responses throughout the liturgy, but there are no musical instruments—just voices. During the liturgy, people stand, sit, and kneel. Before receiving the Eucharist at Communion, people kiss an icon (a holy picture) and a crucifix, which are on a special table in front of the screen. Then the priest gives the Eucharist—a cube of bread with some wine on it—on a spoon.

Comparing the Liturgies

Use the chart below to list the similarities and differences between the liturgies of the Eastern Church described above and the church you usually attend.

Similarities	Differences

Living My Faith

Faith Summary

The Church has members with different roles and gifts in many places. All are united in beliefs, as expressed in the Apostles' Creed and Church teachings. All share in divine life through grace. A visible sign of Church unity is the pope with the bishops, who are the apostles' successors.

Mitre worn on the head of Pope Pius IX

Words I Learned

clergy   evangelization   laity   priesthood   religious life   vows

Ways of Being Like Jesus

In his public life, Jesus called all people—rich and poor, young and old, leaders and outcasts. *Respect and accept all people.*

Prayer

Jesus, thank you for calling me to be a member of your Church and part of a community that unites people from many places and times.

With My Family

Activity As a family, attend a service that reflects a tradition different from your own, such as an Eastern Catholic church or a liturgy in a different language. Talk about how the service shows diversity and unity within the Church.

Faith on the Go Ask one another: *What is your favorite part of our liturgy? Why?*

Family Prayer *Dear Lord, we are blessed by our differences, which make us unique and wonderful in your eyes. Help us to always see the beauty in our diversity.*

Called to Holy Orders

People such as social workers, teachers, and doctors provide particular kinds of services in the community. What kinds of services do these people provide? In what other ways can people serve their community?

Prayer

Dear God, please bless all those who serve the community. Especially bless the priests who help bring us closer to you.

Sacraments at the Service of Communion

The two sacraments that enable people to devote themselves to the service of others are Holy Orders and Matrimony, the **Sacraments at the Service of Communion.** Holy Orders and Matrimony contribute to the personal salvation of those who receive them. The mission of those receiving these sacraments is service in the Kingdom of God.

A bishop ordains a new priest.

When receiving Holy Orders, men accept an important role in serving the community; they help continue Jesus' presence on earth in the tradition of the apostles. Although priests are leaders, all members of the Church participate in the priesthood of believers through Baptism.

In Matrimony the love between married couples is a reflection of the love of Christ for his Church.

Meet a Saint

Turibius of Mogrovejo (1538–1606) was the bishop of Lima, Peru. Originally from Spain, he went to the Americas to help people in the new Spanish colonies there. As bishop, Turibius helped poor people and defended the rights of natives. He traveled constantly through his diocese to care for his people. He built churches and hospitals and set up the first seminary in the Americas to train priests. He is said to have baptized 500,000 people. Turibius was declared a saint in 1726. His feast day is March 23.

Harbor near Lima, Peru

The Sacrament of Holy Orders

Holy Orders is the sacrament by which men are called by the Holy Spirit to serve the Church.

There are three kinds of participation in the Sacrament of Holy Orders: as bishop, as priest, and as deacon.

- ▶ A bishop receives the fullness of the Sacrament of Holy Orders. He is head of a local church called a diocese. He is also part of the episcopal college, the group of bishops who, with the pope, guide the Church.
- ▶ Priests serve the community in various ways, such as presiding at liturgies, preaching, celebrating the sacraments, and teaching.
- ▶ Deacons serve the needs of the community, proclaim the Gospel, teach, baptize, witness marriages, and assist the priest celebrant at liturgies.

Transitional deacons are studying to become priests. Permanent deacons are called to remain deacons for life.

The Rite of the Sacrament of Holy Orders

Men receive the Sacrament of Holy Orders in the Rite of **Ordination,** by which the bishop, through the laying on of hands, prays a prayer asking the Holy Spirit to give candidates the ability to minister to the Church. Through this rite these men receive a permanent spiritual mark, called a **character,** marking them as representing Jesus' presence in the Church. A new priest's hands are then anointed with Chrism. In the rite for a bishop, the new bishop's head is anointed with Chrism.

Link to Liturgy

After a priest has been ordained, he is vested with a stole and chasuble and his hands are anointed with Chrism. The bishop prays that the priest be preserved in the power of the Holy Spirit to help the people become holy and to offer sacrifice to God.

GO TO PAGE 236

Faith Summary

The Sacraments at the Service of Communion are Holy Orders and Matrimony. Through these sacraments people help serve God's kingdom by service to others. Holy Orders is the sacrament in which men are called to serve the Church as bishops, priests, and deacons.

Words I Learned

basilica   character   ordination
Sacraments at the Service of Communion

Ways of Being Like Jesus

Jesus always prayed with reverence. *Provide a good example by participating reverently in liturgy or helping others learn more about Jesus.*

Basilica at Cartago, Costa Rica

Prayer

Dearest God, thank you for all those who serve the Church. Help me to serve you and to know that I am doing your will.

With My Family

Activity Priests and deacons are part of your Church family. Get to know them better by inviting a parish priest and deacon to share a meal with your family. Ask questions about their vocation and the work they do for the Church.

Faith on the Go Ask one another: *If our priest were here right now, what one question would you want to ask him?*

Family Prayer *Father in heaven, bless those who serve you as leaders in our Church. Be with them and give them strength to know and do your will.*

How is your family like a small community? What activities do you do together? What are your duties? How do you learn from one another? How do you help one another? How do you show your love?

The Domestic Church

Prayer

Jesus, my helper, show me how to love, forgive, and share within my family so that I can help my home be a place where your love can be found.

The Family as the Domestic Church

In Christianity the family has traditionally been called the **domestic church.** In the domestic church, children are introduced to the faith by learning to worship God, to love and forgive, and to work together. Cooperating with the Holy Spirit, the family forms a community of grace and prayer where children practice living a holy life and loving one another.

Maria and Luigi

Luigi Beltrame Quattrocchi (1880–1951) and Maria Corsini Beltrame Quattrocchi (1884–1965) show us how a family forms a domestic church. Married in Rome in 1905, they had four children, three of whom entered religious communities.

Luigi, a lawyer, was an example of dedication to family and work. He was active in serving the community and promoting Christian values. Maria was also active in the community, ministering to people's needs, as well as writing on education, and teaching about God.

This married couple is an example of how to foster an atmosphere of faith in the home and how to serve the community. Although their life was ordinary, they lived it in an extraordinary way. They were the first married couple to be named "blessed" together. Being named "blessed" is a step toward sainthood.

Beltrame Quattrocchi family, 1922.

The Sacrament of Matrimony

God calls couples to a special vocation through the Sacrament of Matrimony: to live a life of love in a community. In this sacrament a man and a woman celebrate their commitment to lifelong love for each other. Matrimony builds the People of God. As a result, like Holy Orders, Matrimony is called a Sacrament at the Service of Communion.

Matrimony is based on the personal decision of a man and woman, who promise to dedicate themselves to each other for their lives. As a sacrament the couple's union is a reflection of the love of Christ for his Church.

Because marriage is important in building the People of God, the celebration of a couple's love takes place before a priest or another witness approved by the Church. In the ceremony itself, the couple exchanges promises. They are the ministers of the sacrament.

Celebrating Matrimony

Matrimony often takes place during the celebration of a Eucharistic liturgy. Here is an example of the kind of promises that couples exchange:

> "I, [name], take you, [name], to be my wife/husband. I promise to be true to you in good times and in bad, in sickness and in health. I will love you and honor you all the days of my life."

Through the Sacrament of Matrimony, couples receive the grace they need to perfect their human love in a way that makes it similar to Christ's love for his Church.

Reading God's Word

. . . wherever you go I will go.   *Ruth 1:16*

GO TO PAGE 237

Mealtime Prayers

A family forms a special community called the domestic church. Part of being a domestic church is praying together as a family.

You can pray as a family before and after meals with the following prayers.

Prayer Before Meals

Bless us, O Lord, and these your gifts
which we are about to receive from your goodness.
Through Christ Our Lord.
Amen.

Prayer After Meals

We give you thanks
for all your gifts,
almighty God,
Living and reigning
now and for ever.
Amen.

We get nourishment, energy, and enjoyment from the foods we eat and from one another's company. All these gifts are from God. Take some time now to thank God for his generosity.

Building the Domestic Church

In Matrimony the Holy Spirit gives a couple the strength of enduring love. The Spirit also helps us to build the domestic church.

Tell how you will live your role in the domestic church.

St. Joseph the Worker, Michael D. O'Brien.

I promise to help make my family a place of prayer by

_____

_____.

I promise to help make my family a place of sharing by

_____

_____.

I promise to help make my family a loving community by

_____

_____.

I promise to help make my family a forgiving community by

_____

_____.

I promise to help make my family a serving community by

_____

_____.

Link to Liturgy

We form a community of prayer when we gather together to celebrate liturgy. A family forms a community of prayer when, for example, it prays grace before and after meals.

Living My Faith

Faith Summary

The Sacrament of Matrimony is based on a man and a woman's promise of lifelong love. The couple receives grace from the Holy Spirit to fulfill their promise. Their union reflects the enduring love between Jesus and the Church. The couple and their children make up the domestic church.

Words I Learned

domestic church

Ways of Being Like Jesus

Jesus loved and cared for all people. *Respect your family and promote love and closeness within it.*

Prayer

Jesus, thank you for letting me be part of a special community of love and prayer with my family. Thank you for putting others in my life so that together we may grow closer to you.

With My Family

Activity As a family, decide on various ways you can make your home a place of prayer, love, sharing, and forgiving. Write your ideas on a sheet of paper and hang it in a prominent place in your home. Refer to it daily and make a commitment to put the ideas into action.

Faith on the Go Ask one another: *What is the most important thing I have learned from being a part of this family?*

Family Prayer *Dear God, bless our domestic church. Help each of us be ministers of love to one another and let us always feel your loving presence with us.*

Think about a time when someone asked you to do a special job or perform a certain task. What skills or talents did you use to do the task? How did you feel about accepting the job? How did you feel when you finished the task?

God Calls Us

Prayer

Jesus, my helper, show me how to love, forgive, and share within my family so that our home will be a place where your love can be found.

Using One's Talents for Service

In the early Church, some people who received gifts from the Holy Spirit did not use them well. As a result, there was disorder in certain communities. Saint Paul wrote to address the problem.

> Now you are Christ's body, and individually parts of it. Some people God has designated in the church to be, first, apostles; second, prophets; third, teachers; then, mighty deeds; then gifts of healing, assistance, administration, and varieties of tongues. Are all apostles? Are all prophets? Are all teachers? Do all work mighty deeds?
>
> *1 Corinthians 12:27–29*

Saint Paul recognizes that Church members have different gifts and roles. He tells everyone to use their talents in the interest of the community and not to make proud displays of themselves. He emphasizes that each person has something to offer the community. Paul goes on to mention that the greatest gift of all is love—a gift that everyone can put into action.

God calls all Christians to a life of mission and service. Some are called to be a priest or a member of a religious community, others to married or single life. Each vocation serves the People of God and God's kingdom.

Reading God's Word

[The] LORD came and revealed his presence, calling out as before, "Samuel, Samuel!" Samuel answered, "Speak, for your servant is listening."

1 Samuel 3:10

The Blessed Virgin Mary's Calling

Assumption of Mary

Mary was called to a special vocation. At the time of the Annunciation, she was called to be the mother of Jesus. By saying yes, Mary cooperated with God in the history of Salvation. She was filled with the Holy Spirit. She received the grace to fulfill her vocation as the virgin Mother of God.

Mary is special among human beings. From the very first moment of her conception in her mother's womb, she was preserved from Original Sin. This is called Mary's Immaculate Conception. She remained totally dedicated to God throughout her life and was free from personal sin.

When Mary's life on earth was completed, after Jesus' Ascension and the coming of the Holy Spirit, she was taken into heaven, body and soul. This is called Mary's **Assumption.** Mary now reigns as Queen of Heaven.

Mary intercedes and prays for us as we work to fulfill the vocations given to us by God. We can ask for her help in prayers such as the Hail Mary and the Rosary.

? Did You Know?

The patroness of the United States is Mary, under the title of the Immaculate Conception.

GO TO PAGE 238

Talking with Mary

God called Mary to be the mother of Jesus. She accepted his call. God has a personal call for you too.

Imagine that you are talking with Mary. Ask her how it felt to be called by God. What does she say to you?

Ask Mary how it felt to say yes to God's call. What does she tell you?

Talk with her about your call to serve. Listen to what Mary has to say to you. What things does she want you to do to serve the community now? Tell her.

Sit quietly with Mary, aware of her love and guidance.

Sharing Talents

God has given each of us special talents and gifts. We are called to share these gifts with others.

A. Write a few special talents and interests that you have.

My talents: _____

_____

My interests: _____

_____

B. Using the ideas from above, write ways you can live Jesus' call now and use your talents for service in each of the following places:

At home: _____

_____

At school: _____

_____

In my parish: _____

_____

In my community: _____

_____

Sacred Site

Mary is the patroness of Cuba, where she is honored as Our Lady of Charity of Cobre. According to legend, in 1600 a statue of Mary appeared at sea to three men in a canoe. She was holding the child Jesus on her right arm and a gold cross in her left hand. The statue itself was fastened to a board that read "I am the Virgin of Charity." As a symbol of Cuban nationality, today images of her bear the colors of the Cuban flag: white, blue, and red. Her sanctuary is now a basilica located in the town of Cobre.

Statue at the village entrance of Cobre, Cuba

Living My Faith

Faith Summary

By our Baptism we are called by the Holy Spirit to serve the community. Jesus asks us to use our talents to serve in specific ways. Mary accepted her vocation as Jesus' mother. She was preserved from Original Sin and remained free from sin throughout her life.

Word I Learned

Assumption

Ways of Being Like Jesus

Jesus served the community and encouraged others to take up their call to contribute to God's kingdom. *Participate in the Mass by reading, altar serving, or bringing up the gifts at Offertory.*

Prayer

Jesus, thank you for giving us Mary as an example for following God's will. Help me follow her example and show God's love to others.

With My Family

Activity Have family members sit in a circle. Go around the circle and take turns naming one talent or gift that you admire in another family member. End by having everyone name one of his or her own talents. Then discuss ways you can each use your talents.

Faith on the Go Ask one another: *Name three strengths or talents you have. How can you use these talents to serve Jesus?*

Family Prayer *Dear Lord, help us follow Mary's example by putting our trust and faith in you. Guide us to use our talents to serve you better in this world.*

Celebrating Christmas

You may think of Christmas as a one-day celebration of Jesus' birth, but Christmas is actually a whole season in our Church's liturgical year. The Christmas season begins on December 25 with the celebration of the Nativity of Jesus. Christmas gives us time to not only celebrate the birth of Jesus, but also to make choices about how we live our lives now that he is with us.

The season includes the Feast of the Epiphany and ends with the Feast of the Baptism of Our Lord on the first Sunday after Epiphany. While it is one of the shortest seasons, Christmas is one of the most joyful and exciting seasons. Ordinary Time follows the Christmas season.

The word *Christmas* comes from the Old English *Cristes Maesse*, which means "Mass of Christ." Today we call it *Christmas* because we celebrate the birth of Christ at Mass.

Prayer

Dear Jesus, welcome! I'm so excited to celebrate your coming into the world. Please be with me during the season of Christmas as I try to live by your example.

We Celebrate God's Gift During Christmas

Christmas is a time of celebration. As we rejoice in the birth of Jesus, we reflect upon the wonderful gift God has shared with us. We seek the inspiration to live in a way that shows how grateful we are for the gift of Jesus.

Christmas is a reminder that we are each called to live a holy life. God's call urges us to action. When we answer his call, we try to follow his commandments. God is there to guide our steps, our words, and our actions so that we may live a holy life.

How Can I Live a Holy Life?

What does it mean to live a "holy life"? Take a moment to think about Jesus and how he lived his life. Jesus sets the perfect example and shows us how we can answer God's call. Use the space below to write some things you can do to live a holy life. Remember, you can pray for guidance to answer God's call to be holy.

_____

_____

_____

_____

_____

Reading God's Word

. . . as he who called you is holy, be holy yourselves in every aspect of your conduct.

1 Peter 1:15

Mass During Christmas

Mass during the Christmas season is filled with excitement, festive decorations, and the sounds of joyful carols and hymns. In addition to celebrating the birth of Jesus on December 25, we also celebrate the **Feast of the Holy Family** on the Sunday after Christmas to honor Mary, Joseph, and Jesus. We also celebrate our own families as we try to follow the examples set by the Holy Family.

What We Experience

When you look around your church during the Christmas season, you'll notice the season's liturgical color—bright white—on the priest's vestments and altar linens. The Nativity scene shows the Holy Family just after the birth of Jesus. You will see Mary and Joseph as new parents preparing to raise their infant child. Mary and Joseph loved and supported Jesus, raising him according to God's will. For this we honor the Holy Family.

The Holy Family Inspires Our Own Family

God graced Joseph's and Mary's lives with the gift of his Son, and they were blessed to have raised Jesus as their child. God also graces our lives with the gift of our own family. Take a moment now to think about a family member who is special to you. Write a letter to God thanking him for that wonderful gift.

_____

_____

_____

_____

_____

Did You Know?

Saint Joseph is the patron saint of fathers.

GO TO PAGE 239

Living My Faith

Faith Summary

Christmas is more than the celebration of Jesus' birthday on December 25. It is a season in the Church's liturgical year when we celebrate many things, including the Feast of the Holy Family. The Christmas season is also a reminder that we are called to live holy lives.

Words I Learned

Feast of the Holy Family

Ways of Being Like Jesus

Jesus was never afraid to keep company with those whom others rejected. *Always show kindness and respect to others, no matter what other people say or do.*

Prayer

Dear God, be with my family and me as we try to follow the example of the Holy Family. Thank you for the gift of your Son, Jesus!

With My Family

Activity When you go to church during Christmas, identify a decoration in church or a part of the Mass that exemplifies the Christmas season for you. Talk about what you see and hear.

Faith on the Go Ask one another: *If you could ask God to help you accomplish one thing during this Christmas season, what would it be?*

Family Prayer Use Christmas as a time to pray together as a family. Say a prayer that God will be with you and that you will be with God when you feel the need to stand up for what you believe in.

Sacraments, Our Way of Life

Saint Bernadette

Bernadette Soubirous was a poor girl to whom Mary appeared in 1858 at Lourdes in southern France. The shrine at Lourdes has been a place for healings and prayers ever since.

Saint Bernadette

Bernadette Soubirous came from a poor peasant family in southern France. On February 11, 1858, while gathering wood, fourteen-year-old Bernadette had a vision of Mary. It was the first of 18 visions she had that year. Mary, who in the visions called herself the Immaculate Conception, asked that people do penance for the conversion of sinners. She also requested that they visit Lourdes, the site of the visions, on pilgrimage. Mary instructed Bernadette to dig for a hidden spring. When she did so, a spring was discovered, and its waters brought healing to many sick people.

Bernadette suffered a great deal as a result of her visions. Many people sought to test Bernadette because they doubted that Mary had ever appeared to her. Others were jealous and treated her unkindly. Through it all, a humble and patient Bernadette steadfastly affirmed the existence of the "lady in white."

Bernadette (center) before becoming a nun

She also recognized that she had received a call to be a nun. Bernadette entered a convent, where she lived a life of holiness and simplicity. In 1876 a new basilica was opened at Lourdes. Bernadette chose not to attend the celebration because she did not want to attract any attention.

Bernadette died at the age of 35 and was canonized in 1933. She was the first saint to be photographed, and in 1943 a Hollywood film was made about her life. Her feast day is April 16.

Grotto at Lourdes, where Bernadette had her visions of Mary

The New Passover

Think about times when you eat with others. At what special events do you share food? What kinds of food do you eat on these occasions? How do you feel when you share food or a meal with others?

Prayer

Jesus, help me see how you give us spiritual food. Help me to be close to you in celebrating the Eucharist with others and in receiving you in Holy Communion.

Passover, the Last Supper, and the Eucharist

Passover plate

Jesus instituted the Eucharist at the Last Supper during the season of **Passover,** the central celebration of the Jewish people. Passover recalls God's liberation of the Hebrews from slavery in Egypt at the time of Moses.

God called Moses to lead his people out of Egypt, but the ruler of Egypt refused to hear Moses's request to free the Hebrews. So God sent the Egyptians a series of plagues, including frogs, flies, and locusts. Finally the angel of God's judgment brought death to the firstborn males of the Egyptians, while "passing over" the houses of the Hebrew families. The Hebrew families had been asked to sacrifice a lamb and place its blood over their doors so the angel would know which houses to pass over. The Egyptian ruler finally relented and let the Hebrews go.

This event is celebrated in the Passover meal. At the meal Jewish people view God's liberating acts as taking place not just in the past but also in their own lives.

Christians see the story of Passover as anticipating the events of the Last Supper and of Jesus' Passion. The Hebrews were saved at the time of the first Passover meal by the sacrifice of the lamb. All people are saved by Jesus' sacrifice.

More About Passover

1. Read Exodus 12:3–8. What was eaten at the Passover meal?

   _____

2. Read Exodus 12:3–8,12–13. What were Jews asked to put over their doors to show they followed God?

   _____

The Eucharist as Celebration and Sacrament

At the Last Supper, Jesus provided for our spiritual needs by instituting the Eucharist. At Mass, the priest says, "For this is my Body . . . for this is the chalice of my Blood." The Eucharist is the focal point of Christian life.

The word *Eucharist*, which comes from a Greek word that means "thanksgiving," can refer both to the entire liturgy of the Mass and to the sacrament celebrated at the Mass. The bread, made of wheat, and the wine, made of grapes, are consecrated during the liturgy, and these become the Body and Blood of Jesus Christ, or Holy Communion.

Jesus is present in the Eucharistic celebration in the person of the ordained priest, in the **assembly**—the people present—in the Word proclaimed, and in Christ's Body and Blood.

The Eucharist is the central celebration in the life of Catholic Christians. Because of the central importance of the Eucharist in their lives, Catholics are obliged to attend Mass on Sundays and on Holy Days of Obligation. The Eucharist is offered for the living as well as for the dead.

Link to Liturgy

We pray the Lamb of God at the Breaking of the Bread, just before Holy Communion. Through it we thank God for sending a Savior, and we praise God's power to forgive our sins and give us peace.

GO TO PAGE 240

Jesus Feeds the Crowd

Recall the story in Mark 6:34–44 of Jesus feeding the crowd with loaves and fish.

Imagine you are in the crowd when the disciples distribute the food. You are sitting on the grass. You eat and are filled.

You notice that there are many baskets of food left over, even though there had been only a few loaves of bread and some fish to begin with.

What goes through your mind?

Then you hear Jesus say, "I am the bread of life; whoever comes to me will never hunger, and whoever believes in me will never thirst."

What is Jesus saying? Think about his words and about who he is.

Someone has come to sit next to you. It is Jesus. He smiles, says your name, and asks, "What do you want to talk about?"

Tell Jesus whatever is in your heart. He is listening. What does he tell you? Thank Jesus for his help.

Feeding and Being Fed

In this session's prayer, you had a chance to think about being part of the crowd that Jesus fed. Reread the story in John 6:1–15 and think about what Philip and Andrew were going through. After reading, take a moment to imagine what this experience might have been like for the disciples. Answer the following questions.

1. What do you do when you notice the hungry crowd?

   _____

   _____

2. Jesus tells you to bring the loaves and fish. What thoughts run through your mind?

   _____

   _____

3. Jesus blesses the food. Now you arc passing it out. Write a few sentences describing the scene. How do the people respond? What do you say to them?

   _____

   _____

   _____

4. The crowd learns that their efforts, when blessed by God, are enough. Are there times in your life when you feel you have nothing to offer or nothing to give? On a separate sheet of paper, write a short prayer telling Jesus what you would like to change in the world, and how you can use your talents to make a difference.

Faith Summary

Jesus is the Bread of Life. At the Last Supper, he gave us the Eucharist, which is the source of Christian life. Jesus is present at the liturgy in the priest, the assembly, the Word of God, and in a special way in the Body and Blood of Jesus Christ.

Jesus and the disciples at the Last Supper

Words I Learned

assembly   **Passover**

Ways of Being Like Jesus

Jesus was alert to the needs of others and offered help to those who needed it. *Help others just by listening to them, or sometimes you can give time and help even though you haven't been asked.*

Prayer

Jesus, thank you for your gift of the Eucharist that helps me stay close to you.

With My Family

Activity Be responsible with the food your family prepares and eats. Shop and plan this week's meals so that there will be no waste. Begin by using items you already have in your kitchen. If there are leftovers, plan to eat them the next day or use them to prepare another meal.

Faith on the Go Ask one another: *In what ways, other than with food, do we "feed" one another?*

Family Prayer Jesus, bless this family as we share food that feeds our bodies. Help us grow closer to you through the Eucharist, which feeds our souls.

Ceremonies and rituals are a part of our everyday lives. What are some ceremonies in which you have taken part? What is the purpose of these ceremonies?

Celebrating the Eucharist

Prayer

Jesus, help me realize how important it is for me to receive you in the Eucharist. May I always grow closer to you.

Christ's Presence in the Eucharist

During the Mass the priest proclaims the words of Christ: "This is my body. This is the cup of my blood." Through these words and through the power of the Holy Spirit, bread and wine become Christ's Body and Blood. Through the Eucharistic Prayer, Jesus Christ is really present in what was bread and wine. This is called the **Real Presence** of Jesus in the Eucharist. The term used to express this belief is *transubstantiation*. Saint Thomas Aquinas used this term to teach that, while the bread appears to be bread and the wine appears to be wine, they both become the Body and Blood of the risen Jesus. This holy mystery occurs during Mass at the time of consecration.

The Triumph of Saint Thomas Aquinas, Francesco Traini.

The Order of Mass

The Mass is the high point of Catholic life, and it follows a set order.

Introductory Rites

The Mass begins with the Entrance Chant and the Greeting. This is followed by the **Penitential Act,** which is a prayer of sorrow for sins. This may include *Kyrie* (Lord Have Mercy), an acclamation of praise for God's mercy, and *Gloria*, a hymn of praise. It concludes with the Collect Prayer.

Liturgy of the Word

In the readings from the Old and New Testaments, from a book called the *Lectionary*, we hear the story of God's plan for Salvation. Then we hear a story about Jesus' life from one of the Gospels. Next, the Homily helps us understand God's Word and relates it to our lives. At the end of the Liturgy of the Word, we make a Profession of Faith (the Creed) and offer the Prayer of the Faithful to pray for our needs and the needs of the world.

Liturgy of the Eucharist

Presentation of the Gifts and Preparation of the Altar

A chalice for the Wine and a paten for the Bread are placed on the altar. Members of the assembly carry Bread and Wine to the priest or deacon who places them on the altar. The priest concludes with the Prayer over the Offerings.

Eucharistic Prayer

This is the heart of the Mass. During this prayer the words of Jesus from the Last Supper and the invocation of the Holy Spirit change the bread and wine into the Body and Blood of Christ. The Eucharistic Prayer begins with the Preface (a prayer of praise to God) and the *Sanctus* (the Holy, Holy, Holy). At the center of the Eucharistic Prayer is the Institution Narrative, which contains the words of consecration. The assembly responds with the Mystery of Faith. The Eucharistic Prayer concludes with a song of praise to the Trinity.

Communion Rite

At this time we express our unity with God and with one another. The Communion Rite consists of the Lord's Prayer, the Sign of Peace, the *Ecce Agnus Dei* (Behold the Lamb of God), the sharing of the Body and Blood of Jesus Christ as a community, and the Prayer after Communion.

Concluding Rite

The Concluding Rite consists of a Greeting, a Blessing from the priest and the Dismissal. It sends us forth on our mission as Catholics.

GO TO PAGE 241

The Eucharist

We adore Jesus Christ in the Eucharist, where our faith tells us Christ is really present. The following prayer expresses adoration of Christ in the Eucharist. This prayer is called *Tantum Ergo*. It is the last part of the *Pange Lingua*, written by Saint Thomas Aquinas.

Tantum Ergo

With heads bowed let us now worship a sacrament so great;
And let the old teaching give way to the new;
Let faith reinforce our belief where the senses cannot.

To the Father and the Son let there be praise and jubilation,
Salvation, honor, virtue, and also blessing;
To the Holy Spirit let there be equal praise.

Many say that seeing is believing. But we can believe without seeing. Think about things you believe in even though you can't touch, see, or hear them.

Talk to Jesus. He is with you right now waiting for your questions. Talk to him about your faith or about something else that is in your heart. Ask him any questions you may have. Listen for his answers.

Thank Jesus for spending time with you.

Identifying the Parts of the Mass

In this session you learned that there are four main parts of the Mass: Introductory Rites, Liturgy of the Word, Liturgy of the Eucharist, and a Concluding Rite. At each of these points, there are specific prayers, gestures, and actions.

A. Look at the following list. Write the part of the Mass in which each occurs: Introductory Rites **(I)**, Liturgy of the Word **(W)**, Liturgy of the Eucharist **(E)**, or Concluding Rite **(C)**.

1. _____ Mystery of Faith

2. _____ the words *This is my Body*

3. _____ Collect Prayer

4. _____ Dismissal

5. _____ Sign of Peace

6. _____ Gospel

7. _____ *Gloria*

8. _____ Profession of Faith

9. _____ *Sanctus*

10. _____ Homily

Jesus Christ is truly present in the Blessed Sacrament, Elizabeth Wang.

B. Which part of the Mass is the most meaningful for you? Why?

_____

_____

C. Which part of the Mass would you like to understand better?

_____

_____

Faith Summary

At Mass we commemorate, or recall, the sacrifice of Jesus. We celebrate the Real Presence of Jesus under the appearance of Bread and Wine. The liturgy of the Mass follows a set order, which includes Introductory Rites, Liturgy of the Word, Liturgy of the Eucharist, and a Concluding Rite.

Stained glass window, St. Jerome's Church, Minnesota

Words I Learned

memorial*   Penitential Act   Real Presence

Ways of Being Like Jesus

Jesus encouraged his followers to be aware of the presence of God in their lives and pray to stay close to him. *One way for us to do this is by receiving the Eucharist frequently.*

Prayer

Jesus, thank you for your presence in the Eucharist and in my life.

With My Family

Activity On Sunday before you participate in Mass with your family, make a list of the special intentions for which you will pray. Bring your list to Mass. Silently include your special intentions with the Universal Prayer.

Faith on the Go Ask one another: *In what parts of your everyday life do you feel the presence of God? Share some examples or experiences.*

Family Prayer *Heavenly Father, we feel you near to us at Mass. Help us also know your loving presence in the great and small moments of our everyday lives.*

What are some times when you are called on to forgive? Is it easy to forgive? Why or why not?

Celebrating Reconciliation

Prayer

Jesus, help me remember that you are always ready to forgive me when I do something wrong.

Jesus Brings a Healing Presence into Our Lives

During his life Jesus was a healer. He worked many miracles, or signs and unexplained acts of wonder, such as healing sick people. Miracles show God acting in the world.

This healing is continued in the Church through the power of the Holy Spirit. It is continued particularly in the **Sacraments of Healing**, which include the Sacraments of Penance and Reconciliation and of the Anointing of the Sick.

The Meaning of Sin in Our Lives

We are in need of healing because of the existence of sin in our lives. Every day we make decisions about whether to live in harmony with God and with others. We can destroy this harmony and break our relationships by acts of disobedience and self-centeredness. Sin is an offense against God.

Totally rejecting God and others in our lives is a grave, or mortal, sin. When the rejection is not so total or serious, it is a venial sin. Continually committing venial sins gets us in the habit of saying no to God and can lead to mortal sin.

God calls us to repentance in the Sacrament of Reconciliation. When we repent because we love God above all, it is called perfect contrition. When we repent for other reasons—for example, the fear of hell—it is called imperfect contrition. By accepting the grace to repent and celebrate the Sacrament of Reconciliation, we can live in peace with God and with others and contribute to peace in the world.

Mural of Christ (detail), Devon Cunningham.

The Sacrament of Reconciliation

The essential parts of the Sacrament of Reconciliation are contrition, confession, satisfaction made by the penitent (the person confessing sins), and the absolution by the priest, who is sworn to keep in confidence what he has been told. *Contrition* means being sorry for sins; *confession* means telling one's sins; *satisfaction* means doing what is possible to repair the harm a sin has caused to another person and to yourself. *Absolution* is the forgiveness we receive from God through the priest.

The Rite of Reconciliation

Before confessing their sins, penitents make an examination of conscience. They think of how they have done wrong or failed to do good. They can ask the Holy Spirit to help them make a good confession. When a person confesses sins to a priest, here is the typical process:

1. The penitent prays the Sign of the Cross.
2. The priest invites the penitent to trust in God. The priest may also read from Scripture.
3. The penitent confesses his or her sins. Grave or mortal sins must be confessed. The priest may help and counsel the penitent. The priest gives the penitent a penance to perform, which is often in the form of an action to complete or prayers to pray.
4. The penitent expresses sorrow for sins, usually by reciting the Act of Contrition.
5. The priest gives absolution, using special words that include "Through the ministry of the Church may God give you pardon and peace and I absolve you from your sins in the name of the Father, and of the Son, and of the Holy Spirit." The penitent responds, "Amen."
6. At the end the priest and penitent praise God for his mercy. Then the priest dismisses the penitent with words such as these: "The Lord has freed you from your sins. Go in peace."

GO TO PAGE 242

Saying Sorry to God

You pray the Act of Contrition when you celebrate the Sacrament of Reconciliation. In this prayer you tell God you are sorry for having done wrong. Pray this prayer now slowly, thinking about the words as you say them.

Act of Contrition

My God,
I am sorry for my sins with all my heart.
In choosing to do wrong
and failing to do good,
I have sinned against you
whom I should love above all things.
I firmly intend, with your help,
to do penance,
to sin no more,
and to avoid whatever leads me to sin.
Our Savior Jesus Christ
suffered and died for us.
In his name, my God, have mercy.

God is happy to forgive your sins. He wants you to be close to him. He can help you avoid those things that lead you to sin. Ask God how you can avoid them. What does he tell you?

Perhaps you have your own words to tell God you are sorry for your sins. If you do, try using them now to make your own prayer for forgiveness. Sit quietly and be aware of God's love.

Forgiveness in the Gospels

You have learned about forgiveness in this session. Now read the Parable of the Forgiving Father from the Gospel of Luke (15:11–24). Complete the activity.

In your own words, tell what this passage is about.

Window of Forgiving
Father parable, Corpus
Christi Church, Ontario

_____

_____

_____

_____

_____

_____

_____

_____

What does the passage teach you about forgiveness?

_____

_____

_____

_____

Reading God's Word

If you forgive others their transgressions, your heavenly
Father will forgive you.

Matthew 6:14

Living My Faith

Faith Summary

In the Sacrament of Penance and Reconciliation, we can heal our relationships with God and with others by being sorry for our sins, confessing them to a priest, receiving absolution, and trying to do better. Accepting the grace to repent will help us bring peace and forgiveness to the world.

Words I Learned

Sacraments of Healing

Ways of Being Like Jesus

Jesus brought peace and forgiveness into the world. *Keep an open mind when talking with those who have done wrong to us.*

Prayer

Jesus, thank you for forgiving me when I do wrong. Thank you for helping me be at peace with myself, with others, and with you.

With My Family

Activity Praying for people helps us forgive them. With your family make a Forgiveness Box. Write prayers for those people who have angered or wronged you. Ask God to bless these people. Place these prayers in the box and continue to pray for the strength to forgive.

Faith on the Go Ask one another: *What do you think the world would be like if everyone lived in peace and harmony? How might things be different?*

Family Prayer Loving Father, your forgiveness is a gift. Help us be truly sorry for our sins and remember to share your gift by forgiving those who hurt us.

What does it mean to be healed? How have others acted as healers for you? How can you bring healing to others?

Jesus Heals Us

Prayer

Jesus, help me see how you have brought healing to the world through the sacraments.

Jesus Heals and Saves

The name *Jesus* means "God saves." The name emphasizes that Jesus is the one who has come to save all. *Christ* means "anointed one." The name shows that God the Father has given Jesus a mission and endowed him with power to save and power to heal. Jesus' whole life was aimed at saving people. His words and actions are the foundation of the saving grace we now receive in the sacraments.

The sacrament that helps unite those who are suffering with Jesus' saving and healing power is the Anointing of the Sick. Through this sacrament people receive forgiveness for their sins and comfort in their suffering. They are restored in spirit and sometimes they even experience the return to physical health. The sacrament teaches us that God wants us to give comfort to those who are suffering and wants us to work to relieve suffering where we can.

Sacred Site

Mary appears to Bernadette Soubirous in a grotto at Lourdes.

Lourdes, in southern France, is where Mary appeared to Bernadette Soubirous in 1858 and where many people have experienced healings of various kinds. The Church officially recognizes more than 60 of these healings as miraculous after having subjected them to rigorous medical study. Some people leave their crutches as evidence of their cure. Some bathe in the waters of the spring in the grotto where Mary appeared, and many drink the water in hopes of a cure. About six million pilgrims visit Lourdes every year.

The Sacrament of the Anointing of the Sick

In the Sacrament of the Anointing of the Sick, the priest anoints with the oil of the sick those who are seriously ill, injured, or aged.

In addition to the anointing, the person is often offered Holy Communion. When the person is dying, Holy Communion is called **viaticum.** For a person who is dying, the sacrament is preparation for passing over to eternal life.

Anointing sometimes occurs in a church and is given to people who are sick or aged in a community. It often takes place in homes, nursing homes, and hospitals. For example, a person who is going to have surgery may be anointed. This sacrament may be received more than once, such as when a person who is sick has a condition that worsens.

Priest's travel kit with oil for anointing those who are sick

The Rite of the Anointing of the Sick

In the Rite of the Anointing of the Sick, the priest anoints the sick person on the forehead, saying, "Through this holy anointing may the Lord in his love and mercy help you with the grace of the Holy Spirit. Amen." He also anoints the sick person on the hands, saying, "May the Lord who frees you from sin save you and raise you up. Amen."

The "raising" refers to spiritual healing, as well as to any physical healing that may take place.

Did You Know?

The oil of the sick is a special oil used for the Sacrament of the Anointing of the Sick. The bishop blesses this oil at the Chrism Mass during Holy Week.

GO TO PAGE 243

Prayers for Healing

Jesus heals us and helps us. He healed many people during his life on earth. He brought Jairus's daughter back to life and cured the man who was paralyzed from birth. Jesus continues to heal and help us today.

Imagine that you are walking with Jesus. As you walk you see people who are sick, suffering, grieving, disappointed, lonely, and excluded. You may know some of the people.

How do you think Jesus looks at these people? What does he feel toward them? What do you think he says to them? How does he bring comfort to them?

Take a while and talk to Jesus. Tell him what you thought about the people you passed. Ask him to help you find ways to help them.

You might need some help or healing yourself. If you do, ask Jesus for it.

Listen for his answer.

Comparing the Two Sacraments of Healing

The following statements are about the Sacraments of Reconciliation and the Anointing of the Sick. Identify which statements are true and which are false by placing a **T** or an **F** on the line. Look back at Session 18 if needed.

1. _____ The priest may never repeat what the penitent has confessed.

2. _____ The Act of Contrition is used to express joy and to praise God.

3. _____ The Sacrament of the Anointing of the Sick is only for those who are near death.

4. _____ The absolution by the priest is one of the essential parts of the Sacrament of Reconciliation.

5. _____ *Contrition* means being sorry for your sins.

6. _____ The Holy Communion offered to a dying person is called viaticum.

7. _____ In the Rite of the Anointing of the Sick, the priest anoints the sick person on the forehead and the hands.

8. _____ Before confessing sins the penitent makes an examination of conscience.

9. _____ The Anointing of the Sick takes place only in church.

10. _____ The Sacrament of the Anointing of the Sick may be received only once.

Living My Faith

Faith Summary

In the Sacrament of the Anointing of the Sick, the priest uses oil to anoint those who are ill, injured, or aged. As a result they receive forgiveness for their sins, comfort in their suffering, and spiritual healing. Through this sacrament we are united with Jesus in his Passion and Death. We participate, through our suffering, in his saving and healing work.

Stained-glass window showing oil for the Anointing of the Sick

Word I Learned

viaticum

Ways of Being Like Jesus

During his life Jesus showed special sympathy to those who were sick. He healed the sufferings of many. *Show concern for people who are sick and help them by comforting them or befriending them.*

Prayer

Jesus, thank you for your healing presence in our lives. Help me to see other people through your loving eyes.

With My Family

Activity With your family, make a few fun, colorful cards for some of the children who are sick at a hospital. Bring the cards to the hospital to be distributed by a volunteer.

Faith on the Go Ask one another: *If you could heal someone who is hurting, whom would it be? Why?*

Family Prayer *Jesus our Savior, touch our lives with your healing hand. Give us strength in our difficult moments and help us to always remember that you are near.*

Celebrating Lent and Holy Week

Lent is the Church season of 40 days in which we prepare for the celebration of Easter. It is a time of reflection, increased prayer, and self-denial.

Lent begins with Ash Wednesday and ends during Holy Week on Holy Thursday. On Ash Wednesday we receive ashes on our foreheads as an expression of sorrow for our sins.

There are three Lenten practices that help us prepare for Easter. First, we can pray more frequently and engage in reflective conversation with God. Second, Lent is also a time of fasting. The Church tells adults to fast from meals and not eat meat on certain days during Lent. Third, we can help those less fortunate by donating our money and time to organizations or the community. This is called almsgiving. These practices help us prepare for Holy Week and Easter, remembering the time when Jesus sacrificed his life for us and was raised from the dead.

Prayer

Dear Jesus, I know you will be with me during the season of Lent. Open my heart to hear your Word and follow your example.

The Passion of Jesus

Holy Week is the last week of Lent. It begins with Passion Sunday, or Palm Sunday. Palms are blessed and distributed to the assembly to remember Jesus' triumphal entrance into Jerusalem. The story of Jesus' **Passion** and Death is read as the Gospel reading. The blessed palms are taken home as a reminder that Jesus is our King.

The Last Supper (detail), Vicente Juan Macip, 16th century.

Lent ends on Holy Thursday evening. We then celebrate the Easter Triduum (three days) on Holy Thursday, Good Friday, and Holy Saturday. During these days we journey with Jesus from his Last Supper through his Death to his Resurrection.

On Holy Thursday we celebrate the Mass of the Lord's Supper. At the Last Supper, Jesus gave himself to us as spiritual food in the Eucharist. On Good Friday we commemorate the day Jesus suffered and died. It is called *good* because Jesus saved the world from sin and death on this day.

The events that led to Good Friday began at the end of the Last Supper. Jesus and his disciples went into the garden to pray. Jesus prayed for strength in the face of his ordeal. Jesus was first questioned by the Temple authorities, then by the Roman governor, Pontius Pilate, who condemned Jesus to death by crucifixion. After hours of suffering, having forgiven his persecutors, Jesus gave up his spirit and died. Jesus' sacrificial death won Salvation for all.

Stations of the Cross

The 14 Stations of the Cross represent events from the Passion of Jesus. We take a moment at each station to think about what Jesus was going through. In prayer we thank Jesus for all he did for us. We ask for the strength and courage to live our lives as his followers.

Reading God's Word

A large crowd of people followed Jesus, including many women who mourned and lamented him. *Luke 23:27*

Mass During Lent and Holy Week

When you go to Mass during Lent, you hear readings that set the stage for Jesus' suffering and Death. Mass is not celebrated on Good Friday, however, because it is the day Jesus suffered and died. Instead there is a service consisting of a Liturgy of the Word, the Veneration of the Cross, and Holy Communion.

What We Experience

During Lent, Mass is more reflective. We do not sing the *Gloria* or the Alleluia, putting them aside until Easter. The Church is adorned in purple, the color of penance. On Good Friday, the church is quiet and somber. The priest wears red vestments, and the altar is free of any decorations or flowers. The crucifix is also draped in red. Part of the Good Friday service is called the Veneration of the Cross. *Venerate* means "to show reverence and respect." A cross is presented for parishioners to reverence with a kiss or a touch to show our respect for Jesus' sacrifice.

The Great Sacrifice

The Veneration of the Cross acknowledges Jesus' great sacrifice for us. Because he died for us, God forgave our sins. As we approach the cross with solemn respect, we realize that we have been saved because of Jesus' suffering and death. Fill in the box below with words and phrases that describe the dual meaning of the cross.

Sorrow	Redemption

GO TO PAGE 244

Living My Faith

Faith Summary

Lent and Holy Week are a time to remember the Passion of Jesus. We solemnly reflect on Jesus' suffering and Crucifixion. The Veneration of the Cross, part of the Good Friday liturgy, symbolizes our reverence for Jesus' ultimate sacrifice and our acknowledgment that the cross is also our way to Salvation.

Church fresco of Jesus (detail), Tilburg, Holland.

Word I Learned

Passion

Ways of Being Like Jesus

Jesus loved us so much he gave his life for us. *Do something selfless for someone you love, such as offering to help them instead of playing games.*

Prayer

Dear Jesus, help us to fully understand the gift you have given us. Be with us as we ready ourselves to live anew with you at Easter.

With My Family

Activity When you go to Mass during Lent and Holy Week, look around your church and find examples of the details described on page 119. Talk about what you see.

Faith on the Go Ask one another: *What is one thing you can do to unite yourself with Jesus' suffering this Lent?*

Family Prayer Invite family members to take turns praying for one another this week.

Morality, Our Lived Faith

Saint Isaac Jogues

Isaac Jogues, a French Jesuit, was one of a number of Christian missionaries martyred in the Americas. He was convinced that his call to service was to teach Native Americans about Jesus.

Saint Isaac Jogues

Saint Isaac Jogues, Jim Lewis.

Isaac Jogues (1607–1646) was educated in Jesuit schools in France and chose to dedicate his life to God by becoming a Jesuit priest. He had a great desire to spread the Gospel to the Americas, and in 1636 he was sent to work in what is now Canada and the northeast United States.

He learned the language of the Hurons, a Native American nation, and traveled as far west as Lake Superior. Missionary work was difficult because of different languages, food, customs, and religious practices. Conflicts among various Native American nations made the work even harder.

During one mission the Mohawks captured Isaac Jogues, René Goupil, a lay worker trained in medicine, and a number of Hurons. Nevertheless, Isaac Jogues continued to preach and tend to others' needs throughout his captivity and enslavement. He eventually escaped and went back to France.

As a result of injuries to his hands, Isaac Jogues could no longer hold the host and had to be given special permission to say Mass. Although he could have stayed in France, Isaac Jogues was convinced that his mission was in the Americas and chose to go back. Not long after his return, Isaac Jogues and his companion, Jean de la Lande, were recaptured and then martyred for their faith.

Isaac Jogues and his lay companions René Goupil and Jean de la Lande were declared saints in 1930. Their feast day is October 19.

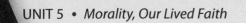

What choices do you have to make in your everyday life about doing what is right? What choices do you have to make to avoid doing wrong?

Making Moral Decisions

Prayer

Jesus, I want to learn how to follow you. Give me the strength and courage to make choices that bring me closer to you.

Putting Our Lives on a Firm Foundation

In the Gospel of Matthew, Jesus uses a forceful image to tell us the importance of having him as the foundation of our lives.

> "Everyone who listens to these words of mine and acts on them will be like a wise man who built his house on rock. The rain fell, the floods came, and the winds blew and buffeted the house. But it did not collapse; it had been set solidly on rock. And everyone who listens to these words of mine but does not act on them will be like a fool who built his house on sand. The rain fell, the floods came, and the winds blew and buffeted the house. And it collapsed and was completely ruined."
>
> *Matthew 7:24–27*

This passage makes it clear that we need to make Jesus central in our lives by following his teachings and trying to be like him. Jesus compares those who follow his teachings to a house on a firm foundation—the storms may come, but believers can withstand the danger. They know that they are friends with Jesus. Those who ignore Jesus' teachings as handed down by the Church or who do not act on them discover there is little to help them when the storms of life come upon them.

Did You Know?

You have an inner voice, your conscience, where you can be alone with God. Your conscience is what helps you decide if an action is right or wrong. You develop it throughout your lifetime with the help of the Scriptures, the Gifts of the Holy Spirit, the advice of others, and the teachings of the Church. When you have a decision to make, taking quiet time alone with God can help you hear the voice of your conscience.

Making Choices

As believers in Jesus Christ, we are called to a new life and asked to make moral choices that keep us close to God. With the help and grace of the Holy Spirit, we can choose the ways to act to stay close to God, to help other people, and to be witnesses to Jesus in the world.

Making good choices and acting on them is not always easy. The right choices are often not clear. Sometimes we are pressured by other people to do something we may not feel is right. At times we may just want to go along with the crowd, whether they are doing right or wrong. When your conscience tells you the right thing to do, you must follow it.

There are certain things you can do to help you decide how God wants you to act. You can:

- ask the Holy Spirit for help.
- think about God's law and the Church's teaching.
- think about what will happen as a result of your decision. When you think about the consequences, ask yourself, will they make you closer to or further from God? Will they hurt someone else?
- ask for advice from people who live the faith.
- remember Jesus Christ is with you.
- think about how your decision will affect your life with God and others.

GO TO PAGE 245

God Helps Us Make Choices

We are faced with choices every day. What should I wear? Do I want milk or lemonade? Should I see this movie or that one? Many of our choices are fairly easy to make. But some of them are harder; some of them are choices between doing right or wrong.

Invite Jesus to be with you while you reflect.

When have you faced a hard choice about doing right or wrong? What happened?

If you think you made the right decision, thank Jesus for giving you the knowledge and courage to do the right thing.

If you think that you made the wrong choice or did the wrong thing, tell Jesus you are sorry. Think about other choices you could have made or what would have helped you make a better choice. Tell Jesus your thoughts.

You know that you can trust Jesus to help you make good choices. Ask him for his help.

Listen in your heart for his answer.

Making Choices: Roundtable Discussion

With a group or by yourself, read the problems below and discuss the choices. Next, decide on one or two good courses of action for the problem. Then present your ideas to the larger group. Be open to discussing the solutions presented by other children in the group.

1. One day some of your friends decide that it would be fun to try to steal something from a store. Each of you is supposed to take something. You don't want to lose your friends or be excluded.

   _____

   _____

2. You want to watch a big game on TV tonight, but you haven't done a report that's due tomorrow. Your brother's report is on the computer. You know you could use it, and no one would ever know that it wasn't yours.

   _____

   _____

3. A classmate in school has a cool, new cell phone—and brings it to school to show off. Your friend takes the cell phone, secretly shows it to you, and brags about taking it.

   _____

   _____

Reading God's Word

When the tempest passes, the wicked man is no more; but the just man is established forever. *Proverbs 10:25*

Faith Summary

As Christians we are called to make moral choices that influence our relationships with God and others. We each have a conscience that helps us with the choices we make. The Word of God, the Gifts of the Holy Spirit, the advice of others, and the teachings of the Church form our consciences.

Word I Learned

habit*

Ways of Being Like Jesus

Jesus made good choices even when it was difficult. *Choose what you know is right, even when the choice is difficult or unpopular.*

Prayer

Jesus, thank you for being with me and helping me to make the right choices.

With My Family

Activity Set aside time once a week to have a family meeting. Discuss personal experiences that family members have had during the week, especially those that deal with making moral choices. Work through problems together and offer suggestions for the future.

Faith on the Go Ask one another: *When have you had to make a difficult choice? How did you come to your decision?*

Family Prayer *Heavenly Father, the world offers us many choices. Help us know right from wrong. Give us strength to act as we should and stay close to you.*

* This word is taught with the Art Print. See page 245.

How do others' words affect you? How do you feel when people say good things about you? How do you feel when people criticize and tease you? Have you ever found out that people were saying unkind things about you behind your back? How did you feel?

Living a Moral Life

Prayer

Jesus, help me use my words to encourage and comfort others, to bring goodness and peace.

Moral Choices

As Christians we are called to live moral lives. A moral life commits us to truth in deeds and words. All too often we make selfish and sinful choices that hurt our relationships with God and others.

One sinful choice we can make is to steal. We can steal people's goods or cheat them. We can also steal with words when we talk negatively about others and take away their good reputations.

Sinning Through Words

The Eighth Commandment, "You shall not bear false witness against your neighbor," is about living truthfully. God is truth, and he wants us always to tell the truth. We must keep a balance between what we should say and what we should not say.

Sometimes we say things about someone else that we know are not true. This is called **slander** and is a sin against the Eighth Commandment. Sometimes we say things about someone else that may be true, but we say them only to harm that person's reputation. This is wrong and is called **detraction.** It is also a sin against the Eighth Commandment.

As individuals with freedom to choose, we are responsible for the choices we make. When we sin we are called to repent and to make reparation (to make up for what we've done) as far as we can.

The Positive Power of Words

Write about an experience when words had a good effect on you.

_____

_____

Write positive phrases that you like to hear.

_____

_____

Sin's Social Side

Sin does not just harm us as individuals and hurt our relationships with God. Sin has negative effects on society as a whole. The presence of sin helps explain why there are such things as war, violence, prejudice, crime, drug abuse, and unfair treatment of others.

Besides lying and using hurtful words, our sinful actions can have negative effects on others in additional ways. For example, when we are greedy, we want more than our share. When we act on our greed, we deprive others of their share. If ten children are given ten cookies to share, and one child greedily takes five cookies, the other nine children are left with only half a cookie each. One child's sin of greed has had a negative effect on the other children. This example shows on a small scale how one person's sin can have a negative effect on society. When whole societies are greedy, bad consequences can result on a large scale.

Exploring the Social Effects of Sin and of Doing Good

Work in small groups and find newspaper stories that show the effects of sin. Discuss the kinds of sin they show. Then find stories of people who are peacemakers through their words or actions. Discuss the stories. Write what you have learned from the discussions.

_____

_____

_____

_____

_____

_____

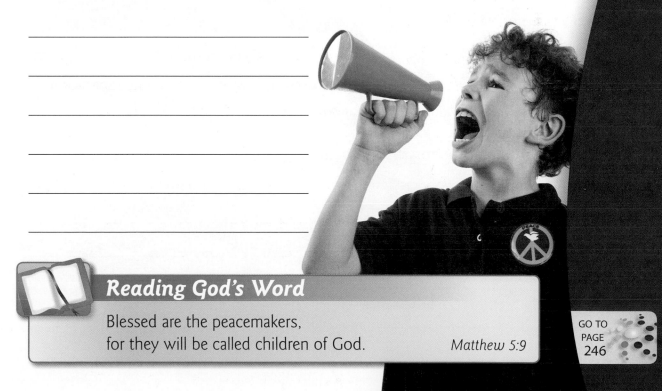

Reading God's Word

Blessed are the peacemakers,
for they will be called children of God.

Matthew 5:9

GO TO PAGE 246

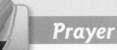

Pray the Psalms

Jesus used words to teach and to heal. His words brought goodness and peace. Pray the following psalm, which is about how we should use our words.

Group One: I will bless the Lᴏʀᴅ at all times;
praise shall be always in my mouth.

Group Two: Keep your tongue from evil,
your lips from speaking lies.

Group One: Turn from evil and do good;
seek peace and pursue it.

Group Two: The Lᴏʀᴅ has eyes for the just
and ears for their cry.

Psalm 34:2,14–16

Let Jesus come to you now. Sit quietly with him for a while. When you are ready, talk to him about using your words for good.

Take some time to think about the things Jesus has told you. Thank him for spending time with you.

Understanding the Psalms

You have read from Psalm 34 about how you should use your words. Part of this psalm is shown again below. After reading it, answer the questions.

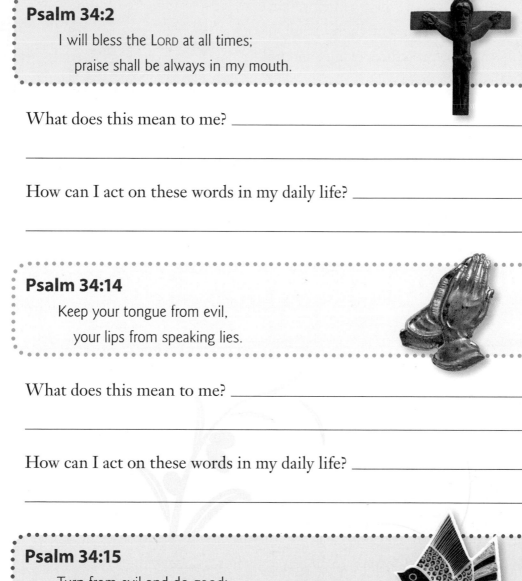

Psalm 34:2

I will bless the LORD at all times;
    praise shall be always in my mouth.

What does this mean to me? _____

_____

How can I act on these words in my daily life? _____

_____

Psalm 34:14

Keep your tongue from evil,
    your lips from speaking lies.

What does this mean to me? _____

_____

How can I act on these words in my daily life? _____

_____

Psalm 34:15

Turn from evil and do good;
    seek peace and pursue it.

What does this mean to me? _____

_____

How can I act on these words in my daily life? _____

_____

Living My Faith

Faith Summary

Christian life commits us to truth in deeds and words. Sin does not just harm us as individuals. It has negative effects on others and on society as a whole. The presence of sin helps explain why there are such things as war, prejudice, crime, and unfair treatment of others.

Gossip, Ile St. Louis, Caroline Jennings.

Words I Learned

detraction

slander

Ways of Being Like Jesus

Jesus used words to help and heal people. *Use kind words to help others see God's love.*

Prayer

Jesus, thank you for showing me ways to use words for good.

With My Family

Activity Around the dinner table, play the game "What Would You Do?" Each family member presents a scenario in which each person responds how they would react in that situation. Discuss what options exist for each scenario and why some solutions are better than others.

Faith on the Go Ask one another: *When did someone's words hurt you? When did someone's words make you feel loved?*

Family Prayer *Dear Lord, help us remember to bless others with our words and in doing so to show our love for you.*

What do you do to take care of your body? What are some ways you see people not taking care of their bodies? What are some things everyone should do to keep their bodies and minds healthy? Share your ideas with the group.

Growing in Holiness

Prayer

Jesus, show me how to love and care for my body and spirit.

We Are Called to Act as Jesus Did

Through the Sacraments, we receive the grace to act in our lives as Jesus acted in his. When we act morally, we reflect Jesus, become his witnesses in the world, and participate in the plan of Salvation. When we live morally, we show our love for Jesus and others.

We Are Called to Act Morally

We learn and live the moral life first in the domestic church, which is our family. Parents care for, love, and respect their children. Children, in turn, owe respect and obedience to their parents. Sometimes it is easy to forget that our parents have busy lives and a lot of responsibility. We can help them by doing what we are told and being helpful around the house.

We can also act morally at school when we respect our teachers and follow rules. We can act morally with our friends when we try to include them and share with them.

Reading God's Word

For I, the LORD, am your God; and you shall make and keep yourselves holy, because I am holy.   *Leviticus 11:44*

We Are Called to Respect Our Bodies

To live a moral life, we need to respect our bodies and ourselves. We can lose control in a number of ways. For example, if we abuse alcohol or drugs or if we dress immodestly, we show a lack of respect for our bodies and ourselves.

As humans we are sexual beings, male and female. God gives sexuality to us; it is part of every person, and it is good. **Chastity** is the practice that helps us unite our physical sexuality with our spiritual nature. It involves respecting our bodies and the bodies of others. United with our spiritual nature, our physical sexuality can be used in the right way. Chastity makes us more complete human persons, able to give to others our whole life and love. All people, married and single, are called to practice chastity. We act in a chaste manner when we practice self-control over our thoughts and actions. In this way we show respect for our bodies. Jesus is a model for chastity.

GO TO PAGE 247

Called to Holiness

Our bodies are part of the goodness of God's creation. Read what Saint Paul says about our bodies. Invite Jesus to be with you as you read.

> Do you not know
> that your body
> is a temple of the
> holy Spirit within you,
> whom you have from God,
> and that you are not your own?
> For you have been purchased at
> a price. Therefore glorify God
> in your body.
>
> *1 Corinthians 6:19–20*

Imagine that you are in a place that is sacred—in a quiet church, in the woods, or by some peaceful stream. It is so quiet that you don't want to speak out loud or make any noise. Feel yourself grow quiet.

Jesus is now next to you. Gently he tells you that you are more sacred than this place.

Reflect on what it means to you to be so special to Jesus.

Seeing Jesus as Teacher and Model of the Moral Life

In the Gospels Jesus both teaches us and shows us how to act morally. Read each of the following passages to learn how Jesus is telling us to act. Then answer the questions.

Jesus prayed for guidance when making moral choices.

Matthew 5:14–16

How does Jesus want us to act?

_____

_____

How can you act that way in your life?

_____

_____

Matthew 5:21–24

How does Jesus want us to act?

_____

_____

How can you act that way in your life?

_____

_____

Matthew 5:43–48

How does Jesus want us to act?

_____

_____

How can you act that way in your life?

_____

_____

Faith Summary

Jesus gives us grace that helps us make good moral choices and act on these choices in our everyday lives. Making good moral choices includes respecting our bodies and practicing the virtue of chastity. Chastity unites our physical sexuality with our spiritual nature and helps us to be complete human persons.

Word I Learned

chastity

Ways of Being Like Jesus

Jesus was respectful to others and remained true to himself. *Be respectful to others and take care of yourself.*

Prayer

Jesus, thank you for giving me the sacraments and through them the grace to make good choices.

With My Family

Activity Make a plan with your family to get some exercise together. For example, take a walk or bike ride through your neighborhood or through a nearby woods or park.

Faith on the Go Ask one another: *Do you have a special place when you want to be alone? What is special about this place?*

Family Prayer *Heavenly Father, let us know the love you have for us. Through the gift of this love, help us to care for and protect our bodies and our minds.*

The Way to Jesus

Who are your neighbors? What does it mean to be a good neighbor? What does a good neighbor do?

Prayer

Jesus, help me be a good, loving neighbor.

The Meaning of Judgment

During our human life, we can either accept or reject God's grace. When we die we will be judged according to our works and faith. As a result of this particular judgment, a person may be united with God in Heaven, may undergo purification in **Purgatory** before being united with God, or, because of his or her choices, may enter **Hell,** which is total separation from God.

Crossing into Purgatory, illustration from Dante's *Divine Comedy.*

In Matthew's Gospel Jesus speaks of the final judgment that everyone will face before God. It describes how all people will need to answer to God for the decisions they have made in life. At the Last Judgment, the Kingdom of God will come into its fullness, and the material universe itself will be transformed. God will then be "all in all."

God intends for all people to live in eternal glory with him. The Church teaches that death was not originally part of God's plan but entered the world through human sin. While in death our souls are separated from our bodies, the soul will be reunited with the body at the end of time.

Link to Liturgy

Vestments worn during funeral rites may be white, violet, or black.

We Pray for Those in Purgatory

Purgatory in Catholic belief is the continuation of the journey to achieve complete union with God—a continuation that occurs after death. The person has been saved and is a member of the Communion of Saints, but the union is still imperfect because of the effect of sin. Purgatory is the final step before complete union with God in Heaven.

As believers we can help ourselves and those in Purgatory on the final journey to God through **indulgences.** Indulgences lessen the punishment due for sins that have been forgiven and are the help we receive to continue to say yes to God and to choose to live the way Jesus taught. Through prayer we also believe that we can intercede with God for those who have died and ask for indulgences on their behalf so that they may be united with God.

To receive an indulgence, a person says a designated prayer such as the Rosary or takes part in a pilgrimage. A person can also receive indulgences for doing good works. The use of indulgences is a voluntary practice in the Church.

Did You Know?

A Holy Year is a special time of joy and pardon. Holy Years occur every 25 years. During a Holy Year, people can earn special indulgences through prayer and visits to churches. Many people make pilgrimages to Rome or to local churches designated as places of pilgrimage.

Young people attend World Youth Day in 2000, the most recent Holy Year.

GO TO PAGE 248

Living the Corporal Works of Mercy

Jesus tells us good ways to treat people. They are listed here from the Gospel of Matthew. Take a moment to reflect on each of these things Jesus calls us to do.

Feed the hungry.

Give drink to the thirsty.

Welcome the stranger.

Clothe the naked.

Care for the ill.

Visit the imprisoned.

adapted from Matthew 25:35–36

Jesus is with you now. Talk to him about the good actions you already do for people. For example, tell him how you feed the hungry or welcome the stranger.

Ask Jesus for help to recognize times when you can do good deeds and show kindness to others. Ask him also for the courage and strength to carry out the actions. Listen for his answer.

Knowing How to Treat Your Neighbor

Think about the ways of treating people that Jesus described in the Gospel story from Matthew. How can you do these same types of things?

Add at least four ideas to the list below.

- ▶ You help to get your little sister ready for school because your mom is busy.
- ▶ You go out of your way to welcome new students in your class and include them in activities.
- ▶ You speak up for someone when others are saying negative things about him or her.

Things I can do . . .

_____

_____

_____

_____

_____

_____

_____

Reading God's Word

For the Son of Man will come with his angels in his Father's glory, and then he will repay everyone according to his conduct.

Matthew 16:27

Faith Summary

After death we will be judged on the choices we have made in life. As a result of this judgment, we will either be united with God in Heaven, undergo a purification in Purgatory before being united with God, or, because of our choices, enter Hell—total separation from God.

Words I Learned

Hell   indulgences   Purgatory

Ways of Being Like Jesus

Jesus befriended the outcast. *Offer friendship and kindness to someone in your class who does not have many friends.*

Prayer

Jesus, thank you for loving me and teaching me how to love you by acting with loving kindness toward other people.

With My Family

Activity As a family, visit a local nursing home or hospital to visit with those who are sick or lonely. Bring books to read aloud or drawings you made as gifts for the recipients.

Faith on the Go Ask one another: *If someone were to write an article about you in the newspaper, what kind acts would he or she describe?*

Family Prayer Lord God, we want to remain close to you always. Help us to make right choices in our lives so that we will live forever in your loving presence.

Celebrating Easter

The season in the Church's liturgical year when we celebrate the Resurrection of Jesus is **Easter.** All the sadness of Jesus' Death on the cross is washed away as we welcome the risen Christ into our lives. The season of Lent ends as we rejoice and sing "Alleluia! Jesus has risen from the dead."

The Easter season begins on Holy Saturday with the Easter Vigil and ends 50 days later on Pentecost Sunday. During this season we also celebrate Jesus' Ascension into Heaven.

The word *Easter* has its roots in ancient times. Many believe that it relates to springtime celebrations and the beginning of new life. Today, when we hear the word, we think of Jesus' Resurrection. Every spring we joyfully celebrate Jesus' victory over death and the gift of new life that it breathes into us.

Prayer

Dear Jesus, thank you for dying for our sins. Help me share your love and peace with everyone I meet.

Our Mission During Easter

We have a **mission** during the Easter season. A mission is a special job given to a person to complete. After Jesus rose from the dead, he spent time with his disciples. In John 21:17 Jesus says to Simon Peter, "Feed my sheep." Jesus tells Peter to serve and care for us, just as a shepherd tends to his sheep. Jesus also calls us. Our mission is to love and serve others.

How can you answer the call? There are many ways to reach out in your own community. Complete each sentence below to tell how you can care for and serve others.

In my school I can _____

_____.

At the local nursing home or hospital, I can _____

_____.

In my own neighborhood, I can _____

_____.

My Mission

How can you be faithful to your mission? You can use the unique talents that God has given you. List your talents below and tell how you can use them to fulfill your mission to love and serve others.

_____

_____

_____

_____

Reading God's Word

For the Son of Man did not come to be served but to serve . . .   *Mark 10:45*

Mass During Easter

The Easter season celebrates Jesus' Resurrection, his Ascension into Heaven, and Pentecost. At Mass we gather as a community and hear all that Jesus said and did. At the end of Mass, we hear "Go forth, the Mass has ended." Now that Jesus has risen and returned to Heaven, we think about how we can carry on his work here on earth.

What We Experience

When you look around your church during the Easter season, you'll notice white altar linens and vestments, white Easter lilies, and bouquets of spring flowers decorating the sanctuary. The blooms are symbols of new life. White, the season's liturgical color, represents joy and victory. The color, beauty, and joy that fill your church during the Easter season celebrate the risen Christ.

Stone mosaic of the resurrected Jesus

Serve the Lord and Others

As you leave church, pick up a bulletin. Take a few minutes to read through it and discover how members of your parish community are answering God's call to serve. Perhaps several members held a clothing drive for children in another country, or another group organized a retreat for young people. Think about a service project you participated in recently. Write about it in the space below.

_____

_____

_____

_____

? Did You Know?

The feast of the Ascension is celebrated 40 days after Easter Sunday, or in some places on the Seventh Sunday of Easter.

GO TO PAGE 249

Living My Faith

Faith Summary

The Easter season begins on Holy Saturday when we remember Jesus' Resurrection. The season continues through the feast of the Ascension, when Jesus ascended into Heaven, and then ends on Pentecost, when God sent the Holy Spirit to Jesus' disciples. Filled with joy and praise, our Church celebrates the risen Christ. It is a time for us to think about our mission to serve others.

Words I Learned

Easter   **mission**

Ways of Being Like Jesus

Jesus gave without expecting anything in return. *Do a nice deed for someone without expecting a "thank-you" in return.*

Prayer

Dear God, thank you for the gift of your Son, Jesus. Help us to serve others as he did—with love.

With My Family

Activity When you go to Mass during Easter, look around your church for decorations described on page 149. Talk about what you see.

Faith on the Go Ask one another: *What do you think might be your mission of service?*

Family Prayer During the Easter season, invite family members to pray together for the president, congressional representatives, the mayor, and other civic officials. Ask God to be with them and guide their hearts and actions as they serve the people they represent.

The Year in Our Church

Liturgical Calendar

The liturgical calendar shows us the feasts and seasons of the Church year.

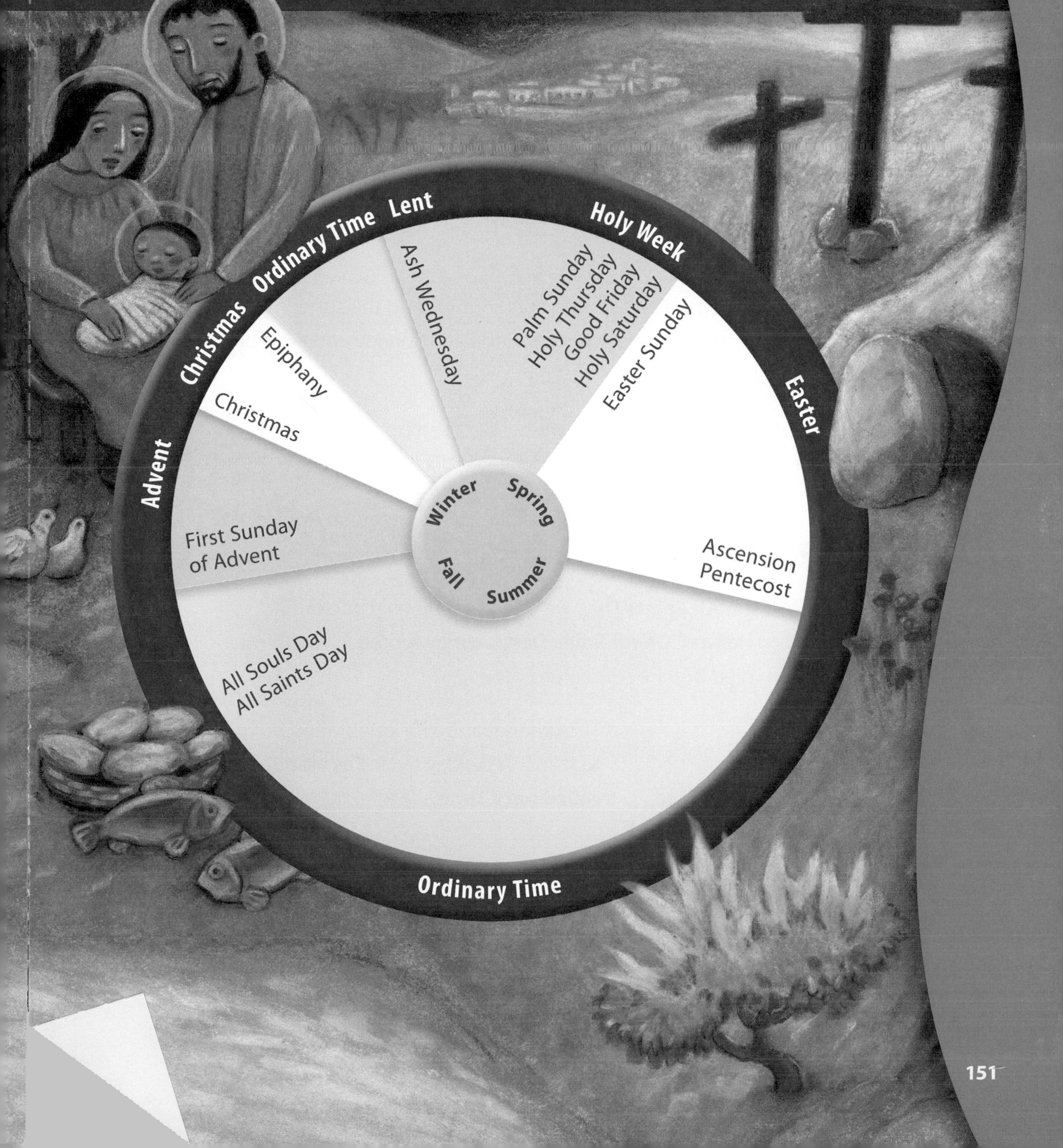

Ordinary Time

Lent

Holy Week

Christmas

Ash Wednesday

Palm Sunday
Holy Thursday
Good Friday
Holy Saturday

Epiphany

Easter Sunday

Christmas

Easter

Advent

Winter

Spring

Fall

Summer

First Sunday of Advent

Ascension
Pentecost

All Souls Day
All Saints Day

Ordinary Time

Liturgical Year

Advent marks the beginning of the Church year. It is a time of anticipation for Christmas and begins four Sundays before that feast.

The **Christmas** season celebrates Jesus becoming known to the world through his birth and Epiphany.

Lent is a season of conversion that begins on Ash Wednesday. It is a time of turning toward God in preparation for Easter.

During **Holy Week,** we recall the events surrounding the suffering and Death of Jesus. Holy Week begins with Palm Sunday and ends on Holy Thursday.

Easter is the time we celebrate Jesus being raised from the dead. The Resurrection is the central mystery of the Christian faith.

The coming of the Holy Spirit is celebrated on **Pentecost.** With this feast the Easter season ends.

On **All Saints Day,** we celebrate the holy persons in Heaven. On **All Souls Day,** we pray for those who have died but are still in Purgatory.

The time set aside for celebrating our call to follow Jesus day by day as his disciples is **Ordinary Time.**

Jesus is the Lamb of God, and we celebrate his sacrifice during Holy Week.

On All Saints Day, we honor Catholic saints, such as Francis of Assisi.

Advent

Advent is a time of anticipation. Although Jesus was born a long time ago, we prepare to celebrate his birth. In the season of Advent, we live in the joyful expectation that his love will grow in each of us in a more complete way.

We prepare to celebrate Jesus' birth so that we will better understand what he means in our own lives. Advent is a good time to reread the Bible stories about Jesus' birth in the Gospels of Matthew, Mark, and Luke, and reflect on ways we can prepare for Jesus.

Prayer

Dear God, help me spend the season of Advent aware of your love so that I will be prepared to celebrate the birth of your Son, Jesus.

Hope for the Future

The events of the Old Testament help us understand what God would accomplish completely in Christ. In 586 B.C. the army of Nebuchadnezzar, king of the Babylonians, attacked and destroyed the city of Jerusalem. Many of the city's Jewish people were exiled to Babylon and forced to live in a hostile land.

The Jews formed their own community in Babylon and remained faithful to God, but as time went by, they began to give up hope. Their defeat and the loss of their land made them start to doubt God's promise to protect them.

The Prophet Isaiah, Pietro Perugino, 16th century, Italy.

To encourage the people, God sent the prophet Isaiah. Through him, God gave them a sense of hope for the future. The prophet said:

> The spirit of the Lord GOD is upon me,
>   because the LORD has anointed me;
> He has sent me to bring glad tidings to the lowly,
>   to heal the brokenhearted,
> To proclaim liberty to the captives
>   and release to the prisoners,
> To announce a year of favor from the LORD
>   and a day of vindication by our God.
>
> *Isaiah 61:1–2*

During Advent the Church turns to the comforting and joyful words of Isaiah to help us live with a sense of hope for our future—a hope made possible by the birth of Jesus.

Handel's Messiah

Every year during Advent, millions of people all over the world listen to George Frideric Handel's *Messiah*. This famous choral work is in three parts: (1) the prophecy and coming of the Messiah, (2) the redemption of humankind through the sacrifice of Jesus, and (3) praise and thanksgiving to God. The work starts with these words from Isaiah:

> Comfort ye, comfort ye my people, saith your God.
> Speak ye comfortably to Jerusalem, and cry unto her,
>   that her warfare is accomplished,
>   that her iniquity is pardoned . . .
> The voice of him that crieth in the wilderness,
>   Prepare ye the way of the LORD, make straight
>   in the desert a highway for our God.
>
> *Isaiah 40:1–3 (King James Version)*

Songs of Praise

Think of a song about Christmas that makes you feel joyful or hopeful. On the lines below, describe how the lyrics of the song convey the Christmas season for you.

_____

_____

_____

_____

_____

_____

All: *O God, we remember your promise to send us your Son. May the blessing of Christ come upon us, brightening our way and guiding us by his truth.*

Leader: *May the Light of Christ shine forth in each of us.*

All: *Amen.*

Reader: *A reading from the prophet Isaiah.*
[Isaiah 61:1–2,10–11]

The Word of the Lord.

All: *Thanks be to God.*

Group A: *O Lord and Ruler of the House of Israel, you appeared to Moses in the flame of the burning bush and gave him the Law on Sinai.*

Group B: *Come, and redeem us with outstretched arms.*

Group A: *O Rising Dawn, Radiance of the Light Eternal and Sun of Justice,*

Group B: *Come, and enlighten those who sit in darkness and in the shadow of death.*

Group A: *O Emmanuel, our King and Lawgiver, the Expected of the Nations and their Savior,*

Group B: *Come, and save us, O Lord our God.*

Leader: *Let us pray in the words Jesus gave us. Our Father . . .*

Go now praising God by your lives.

All: *In the name of the Father, and of the Son, and of the Holy Spirit. Amen.*

Christmas

The birth of Jesus was the birth of God's only Son, the Messiah, who had been promised to the People of God by the prophets of the Old Testament. We celebrate Christmas to remember that God became man in Jesus, while remaining divine.

Prayer

Loving God, help me welcome Jesus into my heart during the season of Christmas.

Epiphany

In the time following the birth of Jesus, many important things happened. The Magi, or wise men, from the East came to Bethlehem to see the newborn king. On their way to Bethlehem, the Magi stopped in Jerusalem and met King Herod, who was the leader of the Jewish people.

Print of Mary and Jesus from an Australian postage stamp.

King Herod felt worried about the birth of Jesus. Herod was afraid that Jesus would become a powerful leader who would threaten the king's own power. According to the Bible, Herod decided to kill the baby Jesus. Herod told the Magi, "After you find the baby, return here and tell me where I can find him, so I can worship him too." The Magi did not trust Herod, however, and returned home without returning to Jerusalem.

Herod was angry and decided on a plan to kill Jesus. However, an angel of God appeared to Joseph in a dream and warned him to take Mary and Jesus and escape to Egypt. When it was safe, Joseph, Mary, and Jesus returned to Israel.

adapted from Matthew 2:1–15

The word *epiphany* means "to show or reveal." During the Christmas season, we celebrate the fact that, in Jesus Christ, God is revealed to us. On the Feast of the Epiphany, we celebrate that day when Jesus was revealed to the whole world, represented by the Magi who came from distant lands. Like the Magi, we come to adore the newborn king and to go forth, carrying tidings of great joy to all those we meet.

The Magi

> May the kings of Tarshish and the islands bring tribute,
>   the kings of Arabia and Seba offer gifts. *Psalm 72:10*

This Old Testament passage led to the traditional interpretation of the Magi as kings. While the Magi are never numbered as three in Matthew's account, the fact that three gifts were offered suggests three gift bearers.

A Gift for Jesus

The Magi gave gifts to Jesus to honor him. You can honor Jesus with a gift as well. You might give him the gift of a special prayer, or you might do something kind or helpful for another person, knowing that when you serve others, you serve Jesus. On the lines provided, write your special prayer or the details of how you will be kind or helpful to another person in Jesus' honor.

_____

_____

_____

_____

Leader: *Let us pray. Jesus, you came to us, our Savior, as the prophets said you would. We rejoice in your presence and pray to always follow your way. This we pray through you with the Father in the Holy Spirit.*

Reader: *A reading from the holy Gospel according to Matthew.*

[Matthew 2:1–12]

The Gospel of the Lord.

All: *Praise to you, Lord Jesus Christ.*

Group A: The people who lived in gloom have seen a great light;

Group B: Upon those who walked in darkness a light has shone.

Group A: For a child, a son, is born to us.

Group B: They name him God, Hero, Prince of Peace.

adapted from Isaiah 9:1–5

Leader: *Let us pray the Lord's Prayer, the words Jesus taught us.*

Jesus has come. As we go forth in his light, let us offer each other a sign of his peace.

Japanese mosaic of Mary and Jesus, Basilica of the Annunciation, Israel.

Lent

During Lent thousands of people all over the world prepare for their Baptisms on Holy Saturday. Throughout these 40 days, the whole Church prepares and prays with them. For example, we read the Bible or go to Mass as often as possible. We repent for our sins and develop good habits. We also help those in need by giving alms or doing good deeds, such as volunteering at a nursing home or donating clothes to charity. By doing these things, we prepare to renew our own Baptism and to honor Jesus' Death and Resurrection.

Lent starts on Ash Wednesday and ends on Holy Thursday. Ash Wednesday is 40 days before Easter, not counting Sundays.

Operation Rice Bowl is sponsored by Catholic Charities during Lent.

Prayer

Loving God, help me spend the season of Lent in prayer and sacrifice so that I will be ready to celebrate the Resurrection of Jesus at Easter.

Christ in the Wilderness, Briton Riviere, 1898.

Jesus in the Wilderness

After Jesus was baptized by John the Baptist, the Holy Spirit led Jesus to the wilderness. In the wilderness Jesus spent 40 days fasting and praying in order for God to make him ready to begin preaching his message of redemption.

After Jesus had fasted for 40 days, he was very hungry. The devil came to him to test him. The devil would tempt Jesus three times. First, since the devil knew that Jesus had to be very hungry, the devil showed Jesus some large stones and said, "If you are the Son of God, command that these stones become loaves of bread." Jesus refused to be tempted.

Second, the devil took Jesus to the top of a high tower at the Temple in Jerusalem. There the devil tried to trick him again. The devil wanted Jesus to jump from the tower so that God's angels could catch him. Again Jesus refused.

Third, the devil took Jesus to the top of a high mountain. He showed Jesus all of the kingdoms of the world. The devil told Jesus that he could be king of all the kingdoms if only he would worship the devil. Again Jesus refused. Finally, Jesus told him, "Get away, Satan." The devil knew that he could not tempt Jesus and left. Then angels came and ministered to Jesus.

adapted from Matthew 4:1–11

Resisting Temptation

The temptation of Jesus contains an important lesson for us: We need to follow God's way and remember to resist temptation. Lent is a time of prayer and sacrifice to help us prepare ourselves to celebrate the redemption offered to us by Jesus' Death and Resurrection. Just as Jesus prepared for his ministry by prayer and fasting, we pray and fast during Lent. We also provide for people who are poor during this time.

Making a Lenten Cross

During Lent we spend 40 days praying, reading the Bible, making sacrifices, resisting temptation, and helping others. To help remember the special activities we do during Lent, make a Lenten cross. Draw a large cross on a sheet of black construction paper. Then cut some small squares from colored construction paper.

Each week during Lent, review the things you have done that week to celebrate Lent. You might have said a special prayer, read the Bible, gone to Mass and Holy Communion, avoided buying candy, given money to charity, or avoided eating meat on Fridays. For each thing you have done, glue one of the colored squares on the cross. Try to cover the black cross completely with colored squares by Easter Sunday.

Prayer Service

Leader: *In the name of the Father, and of the Son, and of the Holy Spirit.*

All: *Amen.*

Leader: *God, as we enter into the season of Lent, help us remember the 40 days and 40 nights Jesus spent fasting in the wilderness.*

Reader: *A reading from the holy Gospel according to Matthew.*
[Matthew 4:1–11]

The Gospel of the Lord.

All: *Praise to you, Lord Jesus Christ.*

Leader: *Let us take time to reflect on the meaning of Lent for our lives. Lent is a time to remember that we are preparing for the celebration of Jesus' Death and Resurrection. Spend a few minutes talking with God about how you will observe this season.*

Thank you for sending your only Son, Jesus, to help us turn from sin.

All: *Help us to grow closer to you through prayer and sacrifice as we prepare for Easter.*

Holy Week

Holy Week is a time for remembering. We remember the events leading to the Death and Resurrection of Jesus.

On Palm Sunday we remember Jesus' triumphant entrance into Jerusalem, and on Holy Thursday we recall how he gave himself to us in the Eucharist. On Good Friday we remember how Jesus suffered and died, and at the vigil Mass on Holy Saturday, we celebrate his Resurrection. Through his Death and Resurrection, Jesus redeemed us from our sins.

Prayer

Faithful God, during Holy Week help me remember that you sent your only Son, Jesus, to die for our sins so that we might be redeemed and live a new life.

Redemption Through Jesus

When Jesus was crucified, two criminals were crucified with him. No one knows the names of the criminals or what they had done. They might have been thieves or murderers. They were put on crosses to the left and to the right of Jesus.

> As they hung on the crosses, one of the criminals cried out to Jesus, "Aren't you the Messiah? Then save yourself and us." But the other criminal interrupted the first criminal and said, "Have you no fear of God, seeing you are under the same sentence? We deserve it, after all. We are only paying the price for what we've done, but this man has done nothing wrong."
>
> Then the second criminal turned to Jesus and said, "Jesus, remember me when you enter your kingdom." And Jesus replied, "I assure you: This day you will be with me in paradise."
>
> *adapted from Luke 23:39–43*

Even in the hour of his Death, Jesus repeated his message of Salvation to the good criminal. Even when he was suffering most, Jesus continued to heal. Because the criminal reached out to Jesus in faith and told Jesus that he believed Jesus' message, the criminal's sins were pardoned.

Jesus' message is the same for us as it was for the faithful criminal: If we believe in Jesus' message of Salvation, we will be redeemed from our sins and find eternal life.

The Last Words of Jesus

The Gospel of Luke records some of the last words of Jesus while he was on the cross. These words show us that even in deep suffering, Jesus stayed close to God and remained loving and forgiving.

Read Jesus' words and think about them. Write answers to the questions.

"Father, forgive them, they know not what they do."

Luke 23:34

What do these words mean to you?

_____

_____

_____

"Amen, I say to you, today you will be with me in Paradise." *Luke 23:43*

What do these words mean to you?

_____

_____

_____

"Father, into your hands I commend my spirit." *Luke 23:46*

What do these words mean to you?

_____

_____

_____

Leader: *As we observe Holy Week, let us remember God's message of Salvation.*

Reader: *A reading from the holy Gospel according to Luke.*

Reader: Now one of the criminals hanging there spoke snidely to Jesus, saying,

Group A: Are you not the Messiah? Save yourself and us.

Reader: The other, however, reprimanding him, said in reply,

Group B: Have you no fear of God, for you are subject to the same condemnation. And indeed, we have been condemned justly, for the sentence we received fits our crimes, but this man hasn't committed a crime.

Reader: Then he said,

Group B: Jesus, remember me when you come into your kingdom.

Reader: Jesus replied to him,

Group A: Amen, I say to you, today you will be with me in Paradise.

adapted from Luke 23:39–43

Reader: *The Gospel of the Lord.*

All: *Praise to you, Lord Jesus Christ.*

Leader: *Let us pray. Jesus, thank you for always loving and forgiving, for healing us no matter what we have done.*

All: *In the name of the Father, and of the Son, and of the Holy Spirit. Amen.*

Leader: *Let us live in peace with one another.*

Easter

Easter is the time when we remember the events in Jesus' life that are most important to our faith: his Death on the cross, his Resurrection, and his Ascension into Heaven. We remember these events each time we celebrate Mass.

The events of Holy Week and Easter are truly amazing. Jesus died for our sins, rose from the dead, and ascended into Heaven. These events are difficult to explain. Not even all of the disciples believed that Jesus had risen from the dead, and some of them demanded proof. We can only believe in the Resurrection through faith.

Painted panel of risen Jesus, Norwich Cathedral, Norfolk, England.

Prayer

Faithful God, help me have the faith to believe your promise to us. You sent your only Son, Jesus, who died for our sins on the cross, so that we might have eternal life.

Jesus Is Risen

After Jesus was crucified, his body was placed in a tomb. On the third day, his body was gone. At first nobody understood what had happened. People felt confused. Then the risen Jesus appeared to many who believed in him. Mary Magdalene and the women who went to Jesus' tomb to prepare his body for burial saw him. So did Peter and many others.

The apostle Thomas, however, was not with the others when they saw Jesus. Later, when Thomas met the others, they excitedly told him the good news: Jesus had risen from the dead and had appeared to them.

Thomas felt surprised and suspicious. He said, "Unless I see the mark of the nails and put my finger into his side, I will not believe."

A week later, Thomas and the apostles were together in a locked room. Suddenly Jesus appeared to them. Everyone felt surprised, because the door was locked. Jesus greeted everyone and then said to Thomas, "Put your finger here and see my hands, and bring your hand and put it in my side, and do not be unbelieving, but believe."

Thomas answered Jesus, "My Lord and my God." Thomas's answer showed that he finally believed. Then Jesus said, "Have you come to believe because you have seen me? Blessed are those who have not seen and have believed."

adapted from John 20:24–29

Believing God's Word

Jesus invited Thomas to touch his wounds on his hands and side. Thomas believed and was saved. Jesus makes the same offer to us. With the eyes of faith, we can see the risen Christ present in ourselves and others. Because of our faith, we believe God's Word and we obtain the Salvation that Jesus won for us on the cross.

Seeing with the Eyes of Faith

When we see with the eyes of faith, we help people who are in need. Our parish community tries to help others. Through various parish ministries, many people bring Holy Communion to people who can't leave their homes because of illness or who are in hospitals. They bring comfort to families that have lost loved ones, or they provide food and shelter for those in need.

You can help people in these ministries by making them cards of thanks and encouragement. On the front of each card, draw a happy-looking face and the words "You See with the Eyes of Faith." On the inside write a note thanking them for their service and encouraging them to continue helping others. When you are finished, your cards will be delivered to people in these ministries.

Site of ancient Middle-Eastern tombs

Prayer Service

Leader:	*Jesus rose from the dead and ascended into Heaven. Through love and service, may we deepen our faith in Jesus and his promise of eternal life.*
Reader:	*A reading from the holy Gospel according to John.* [John 20:24–29]
	The Gospel of the Lord.
All:	*Praise to you, Lord Jesus Christ.*
Leader:	*Knowing that God hears our prayers, let us offer our prayers of petition. The response is Lord, hear our prayer.*
	For all Catholics, that they may be strengthened in their faith in Jesus and his promise of eternal life, let us pray to the Lord.
All:	*Lord, hear our prayer.*
Leader:	*For those who struggle to believe, that their hearts may become open to Jesus and his saving Word, let us pray to the Lord.*
All:	*Lord, hear our prayer.*
Leader:	*Lord, hear these prayers that we speak and the prayers in our hearts. We pray this through Jesus, your Son, and the Holy Spirit.*
All:	*Amen.*

Pentecost

Pentecost icon, St. Maron's Church, Minneapolis, Minnesota.

God sent the Holy Spirit to Jesus' followers on Pentecost. The Holy Spirit gave them the strength and guidance they needed to do God's work. Because of the Holy Spirit, Christianity spread throughout the world. Today the Holy Spirit continues to guide Catholics as we live out our faith.

Prayer

Loving God, thank you for sending us the Holy Spirit that we might have the strength, courage, and guidance to understand and follow your will for us.

A New Follower in Christ

Philip was one of Jesus' early followers. One day an angel of the Lord spoke to Philip, telling him to leave Jerusalem and head out toward the desert. As he traveled he came across a man from Ethiopia.

The Holy Spirit encouraged Philip to approach the man, who was reading the Scriptures. The man began asking Philip questions about the passage he was reading from Isaiah. He asked Philip to explain this Scripture passage:

> Like a sheep he was led to the slaughter,
>> and as a lamb before its shearer is silent,
>>> so he opened not his mouth.
> In [his] humiliation justice was denied him.
>> Who will tell of his posterity?
>>> For his life is taken from the earth.

Philip began talking to the Ethiopian about Jesus. He told him that just like the sheep in Isaiah, Jesus was an innocent victim. Very interested, the Ethiopian asked Philip to get into his chariot so that they could continue to talk as they traveled.

Philip talked more about Jesus. When they came to a stream, the man suddenly asked Philip to baptize him. Philip did so. Prompted by the Holy Spirit, Philip continued his journey, spreading the good news of Jesus. The man resumed his travel back to Ethiopia, rejoicing.

adapted from Acts of the Apostles 8:26–40

Icon (detail) of Philip and the man from Ethiopia, Br. Claude Lane, O.S.B.

Following the Holy Spirit

The Holy Spirit led Philip to complete an important mission—talk to a person from another country about Jesus. Because Philip paid attention to the Holy Spirit, he accomplished a great thing—he proclaimed Jesus' message to a new people in another land. How excited Philip must have felt when he realized Jesus' message was spreading!

The Holy Spirit can lead us to do great things too. He can remind us to help others. He can help us remember to pray for people who are sick. He can help us work hard to be kind to our friends and our brothers and sisters. By being open to the Holy Spirit, we can find out how God wants us to live out our faith and show Jesus' love to others.

The Gifts of the Holy Spirit

As Catholics we believe that the Holy Spirit has given us seven special gifts. These are called the Gifts of the Holy Spirit.

Here is a list of the Gifts of the Holy Spirit. Beside each gift write an example of a way that you could show it in your life today. For example, you might show the gift of counsel when you decide not to repeat a bad rumor that you overheard.

The Gifts of the Holy Spirit

Wisdom _____

Understanding _____

Counsel _____

Fortitude _____

Knowledge _____

Piety _____

Fear of the Lord _____

Stained glass, Sacred Heart
Basilica, Brussels, Belgium.

Prayer Service

Leader: *Let us pray. God our Father, you have sent the Holy Spirit to guide and strengthen us as we follow you. May our hearts remain open to the Spirit. We pray this through Christ our Lord and the Holy Spirit.*

Reader: *A reading from the Acts of the Apostles.*
[Acts of the Apostles 2:1–4]

The Word of the Lord.

All: *Thanks be to God.*

Leader: Lord, send out your Spirit,
and renew the face of the earth.

All: Lord, send out your Spirit,
and renew the face of the earth.

Group A: Bless and praise the Lord our God.
God, you are great indeed!

Group B: How many are your creations, Lord!
In wisdom you have made them all.

All: Lord, send out your Spirit,
and renew the face of the earth.

Group A: If you take away their breath,
they die and return to their dust.

Group B: When you send forth your Spirit, they are given life and you renew the face of the earth.

All: Lord, send out your Spirit, and renew the face of the earth.

adapted from Psalm 104:1,24,29,30

Leader: *Filled with the Spirit, we go to do God's work in the world.*

All: *In the name of the Father, and of the Son, and of the Holy Spirit. Amen.*

All Saints Day and All Souls Day

The Church is like a family. We need to stay in contact in order to remain united. The sacraments, especially the Eucharist, keep us united with God and also with one another. Two feast days—All Saints Day on November 1 and All Souls Day on November 2—celebrate the way that we remain connected and united.

Images from Day of the Dead, celebrated on All Souls Day in Latin American countries

Prayer

Faithful God, as we celebrate All Saints Day and All Souls Day, help me learn how to stay united with you and all those you have saved through prayer and the sacraments.

United in Christ

On All Saints Day and All Souls Day, we celebrate the Communion of Saints. The Communion of Saints includes all the members of the Church because we are all united in Christ.

Jesus used an image of a vine and its branches to explain the Communion of Saints. Vines were common where he lived. A vine is a plant that is very strong and can grow long distances from a single root. From this root grow branches and leaves that are nourished through the vine. When they are attached to the vine, they receive their needed nourishment and are very strong, but they wither and die for lack of nourishment when they are detached.

St. Martin de Porres, Michael D. O'Brien.

Jesus said, "I am the true vine, and my Father is the vine grower. He takes away every branch in me that does not bear fruit, and everyone that does he prunes so that it bears more fruit."

Jesus went on to say, "Remain in me, as I remain in you. Just as a branch cannot bear fruit on its own unless it remains on the vine, so neither can you unless you remain in me. I am the vine, you are the branches. Whoever remains in me and I in him will bear much fruit, because without me you can do nothing."

adapted from John 15:1–5

Jesus emphasizes that we need to stay in contact with him if we are to remain strong as Christians. Through prayer and celebration of the sacraments, our connection with Jesus is strengthened and nourished.

The Communion of Saints

The union of all those, living and dead, saved by Jesus is called the Communion of Saints. Jesus gave us the sacraments, which nourish our faith.

By participating in the sacraments, and especially the Eucharist, we stay close to God and to all other Christians, both living and dead. In the Eucharist all Christians share a deep personal relationship with God. The Eucharist also establishes a union among us, those who have died, and the saints living fully in God's presence in Heaven.

On All Saints Day, we celebrate the Communion of Saints by praying with those who have died and are living in Heaven. We celebrate our union with the saints and all who follow Jesus.

On All Souls Day, we pray for those who have died but are still in Purgatory being prepared to live in God's presence forever. We can help those in Purgatory by praying for them.

Prayers for the Communion of Saints

Write a prayer for someone you know who is alive and needs prayers, and then write a prayer for someone you know who has died.

_____

_____

_____

_____

_____

Saint Thérèse of Lisieux

Knowing and Praying Our Faith

The Bible and You

God speaks to us in many ways. One way God speaks to us is through the Bible. The Bible is the most important book in Christian life because it is God's message, or Revelation. The Bible is the story of God's promise to care for us, especially through his Son, Jesus. At Mass we hear readings from the Bible. We can also read the Bible on our own.

The Bible is not just one book; it is a collection of many books. The writings in the Bible were inspired by the Holy Spirit and written by many different authors.

The Bible is made up of two parts. The Old Testament contains 46 books that tell stories about the Jewish people and their faith in God before Jesus was born.

The New Testament contains 27 books that tell the story of Jesus' life, Death, and Resurrection and the experience of the early Christians. For Christians the most important part of the New Testament is the four Gospels—Matthew, Mark, Luke, and John. The New Testament also contains letters written by leaders such as Saint Paul.

How can you find a passage in the Bible? Bible passages are identified by book, chapter, and verse—for example, Genesis 1:27–28. Sometimes the name of the book is abbreviated. Your Bible's table of contents will help you determine what the abbreviation means. After the name of the book, there are two numbers. The first one identifies the chapter, which in the example below is Chapter 1; it is followed by a colon. The second number or numbers identify the verses, which in the example are verses 27 to 28.

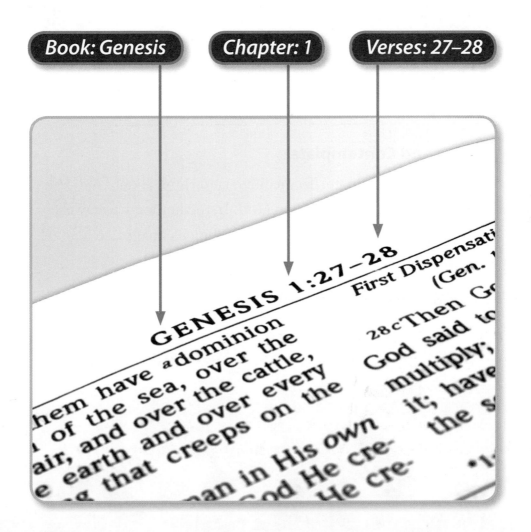

Book: Genesis   **Chapter: 1**   **Verses: 27–28**

Prayer and Forms of Prayer

God is always with us. He wants
us to talk to him and to listen to
him. In prayer we raise our hearts
and minds to God. We are able to
speak to and listen to God because,
through the Holy Spirit, God
teaches us how to pray.

We Pray in Many Ways

Because prayer is so important, the Church
teaches us to pray often and in many ways.
Sometimes we bless or adore God (prayer of blessing
and adoration). Other times we ask God for something
for ourselves (prayer of petition). Sometimes we pray
for others (prayer of intercession). We also thank God in
prayer (prayer of thanksgiving). Finally we can also praise God
(prayer of praise). We can pray silently or aloud. We can pray alone or
with others. Praying with others is called communal prayer.

We Meditate and Contemplate

One way to pray is to meditate. To meditate is to think about God. We
try to keep our attention and focus on God. In meditation we may use
Scripture, prayer books, or icons, which are religious images, to help us
concentrate and to spark the imagination.

Another way to pray is to contemplate. This means that we rest quietly
in God's presence.

We Get Ready to Pray

We live in a very busy, noisy, and fast-paced world. Sometimes, because of this, our attention span can be short. In order to meditate or reflect, we need to prepare ourselves to pray.

We can get ready for meditation by getting our bodies into a comfortable position. Keeping our backs straight and both feet on the floor is a comfortable position. We can close our eyes, fold our hands comfortably in front of us, and slowly and silently take a deep breath and then let it out slowly. We can establish a rhythm by slowly counting to three while breathing in and slowly counting to three while breathing out. We can keep concentrating on our breathing. This will help us to quiet our thoughts.

We Avoid Distractions

If we become distracted by thinking about something, such as the day at school or a sports event, we can just go back to thinking about our breathing.

After a little practice we will be able to avoid distractions, pray with our imagination, and spend time with God or Jesus in our hearts.

Prayers to Take to Heart

We can pray with any words that come to mind. Sometimes, when we find that choosing our own words is difficult, we can use traditional prayers. Likewise, when we pray aloud with others, we rely on traditional prayers to unite our minds, hearts, and voices. Memorizing traditional prayers such as the following can be very helpful. When we memorize prayers, we take them to heart, meaning that we not only learn the words but also try to understand and live them.

Lord's Prayer

Our Father, who art in heaven,
hallowed be thy name;
thy kingdom come,
thy will be done
on earth as it is in heaven.
Give us this day our daily bread,
and forgive us our trespasses,
as we forgive those who trespass against us;
and lead us not into temptation,
but deliver us from evil.
Amen.

Hail Mary

Hail Mary, full of grace,
the Lord is with you.
Blessed are you among women,
and blessed is the fruit of your womb, Jesus.
Holy Mary, Mother of God,
pray for us sinners,
now and at the hour of our death.
Amen.

Morning Offering

My God, I offer you my prayers,
works, joys, and sufferings of this day
in union with the holy sacrifice of the Mass
throughout the world. I offer them for all
the intentions of your Son's Sacred Heart,
for the salvation of souls, reparation for sin,
and the reunion of Christians.
Amen.

Prayer Before Meals

Bless us, O Lord,
*   and these your gifts*
which we are about to
*   receive from your goodness.*
Through Christ our Lord.
Amen.

Prayer After Meals

We give you thanks
for all your gifts,
almighty God,
living and reigning
now and for ever.
Amen.

Act of Contrition

My God,
I am sorry for my sins with all my heart.
In choosing to do wrong
and failing to do good,
I have sinned against you
whom I should love above all things.
I firmly intend, with your help,
to do penance,
to sin no more,
and to avoid whatever leads me to sin.
Our Savior Jesus Christ
suffered and died for us.
In his name, my God, have mercy.

Apostles' Creed

I believe in God,
the Father almighty,
Creator of heaven and earth,
and in Jesus Christ, his only Son, our Lord,
who was conceived by the Holy Spirit,
born of the Virgin Mary,
suffered under Pontius Pilate,
was crucified, died and was buried;
he descended into hell;
on the third day he rose again from the dead;
he ascended into heaven,
and is seated at the right hand of God the Father almighty;
from there he will come to judge the living and the dead.

I believe in the Holy Spirit,
the holy catholic Church,
the communion of saints,
the forgiveness of sins,
the resurrection of the body,
and life everlasting. Amen.

Nicene Creed

I believe in one God,
the Father almighty,
maker of heaven and earth,
of all things visible and invisible.

I believe in one Lord Jesus Christ,
the Only Begotten Son of God,
born of the Father before all ages.
God from God, Light from Light,
true God from true God,
begotten, not made, consubstantial with the Father;
through him all things were made.
For us men and for our salvation
he came down from heaven,
and by the Holy Spirit was incarnate of the Virgin Mary,
and became man.

For our sake he was crucified under Pontius Pilate,
he suffered death and was buried,
and rose again on the third day
in accordance with the Scriptures.
He ascended into heaven
and is seated at the right hand of the Father.
He will come again in glory
to judge the living and the dead
and his kingdom will have no end.

I believe in the Holy Spirit, the Lord, the giver of life,
who proceeds from the Father and the Son,
who with the Father and the Son is adored and glorified,
who has spoken through the prophets.

I believe in one, holy, catholic and apostolic Church.
I confess one Baptism for the forgiveness of sins
and I look forward to the resurrection of the dead
and the life of the world to come. Amen.

Act of Faith

O my God, I firmly believe that you are one God in three divine Persons, Father, Son, and Holy Spirit. I believe that your divine Son became man and died for our sins, and that he will come to judge the living and the dead. I believe these and all the truths which the holy Catholic Church teaches, because you have revealed them, who can neither deceive nor be deceived. Amen.

Act of Hope

O my God, relying on your infinite mercy and promises, I hope to obtain pardon of my sins, the help of your grace, and life everlasting, through the merits of Jesus Christ, my Lord and Redeemer. Amen.

Act of Love

*O my God, I love you above all things
with my whole heart and soul,
because you are all good and worthy of all my love.
I love my neighbor as myself for the love of you.
I forgive all who have injured me and
I ask pardon of those whom I have injured. Amen.*

Hail, Holy Queen *(Salve Regina)*

*Hail, holy Queen, Mother of mercy,
hail, our life, our sweetness, and our hope.
To you we cry, the children of Eve;
to you we send up our sighs,
mourning and weeping in this land of exile.
Turn, then, most gracious advocate,
your eyes of mercy toward us;
lead us home at last
and show us the blessed fruit
 of your womb, Jesus:
O clement, O loving, O sweet Virgin Mary.*

Prayer to the Holy Spirit

Come, Holy Spirit, fill the hearts of your faithful.
And kindle in them the fire of your love.
Send forth your Spirit and they shall be created.
And you will renew the face of the earth.
Let us pray.

Lord,
by the light of the Holy Spirit
you have taught the hearts of your faithful.
In the same Spirit
help us to relish what is right
and always rejoice in your consolation.
We ask this through Christ our Lord.
Amen.

Prayer for Vocations

God, in Baptism you called me by name
and made me a member of your people, the Church.
Help all your people to know their vocation in life,
and to respond by living a life of holiness.
For your greater glory and for the service of your people,
raise up dedicated and generous leaders
who will serve as sisters, priests,
brothers, deacons, and lay ministers.

Send your Spirit to guide and strengthen me
that I may serve your people
following the example of your Son, Jesus Christ,
in whose name I offer this prayer.
Amen.

The Rosary

The Rosary helps us to pray to Jesus through Mary. When we pray the Rosary, we think about the special events, or mysteries, in the lives of Jesus and Mary.

The Rosary is made up of a string of beads and a crucifix. We hold the crucifix in our hands as we pray the Sign of the Cross. Then we pray the Apostles' Creed.

Next to the crucifix, there is a single bead, followed by a set of three beads and another single bead. We pray the Lord's Prayer as we hold the first single bead and a Hail Mary at each bead in the set of three that follows. Then we pray the Glory Be to the Father. On the next single bead, we think about the first mystery and pray the Lord's Prayer.

There are five sets of ten beads; each set is called a decade. We pray a Hail Mary on each bead of a decade as we reflect on a particular mystery in the lives of Jesus and Mary. In some places, people pray the Hail, Holy Queen (*Salve Regina*) after the last decade. The Glory Be to the Father is prayed at the end of each set. Between sets is a single bead on which we think about one of the mysteries and pray the Lord's Prayer.

We end by holding the crucifix in our hands as we pray the Sign of the Cross.

Praying the Rosary

9. Pray ten Hail Marys and one Glory Be to the Father.

10. Think about the fourth mystery. Pray the Lord's Prayer.

8. Think about the third mystery. Pray the Lord's Prayer.

11. Pray ten Hail Marys and one Glory Be to the Father.

7. Pray ten Hail Marys and one Glory Be to the Father.

12. Think about the fifth mystery. Pray the Lord's Prayer.

6. Think about the second mystery. Pray the Lord's Prayer.

5. Pray ten Hail Marys and one Glory Be to the Father.

13. Pray ten Hail Marys and one Glory Be to the Father.

4. Think about the first mystery. Pray the Lord's Prayer.

Pray the Hail, Holy Queen.
Many people pray the Hail, Holy Queen after the last decade.

3. Pray three Hail Marys and one Glory Be to the Father.

2. Pray the Lord's Prayer.

14. Pray the Sign of the Cross.

1. Pray the Sign of the Cross and the Apostles' Creed.

Mysteries of the Rosary

The Church has used three sets of mysteries for many years. In 2002 Blessed Pope John Paul II proposed a fourth set of mysteries—the Mysteries of Light, or Luminous Mysteries. According to his suggestion, the four sets of mysteries might be prayed on the following days: the Joyful Mysteries on Monday and Saturday, the Sorrowful Mysteries on Tuesday and Friday, the Glorious Mysteries on Wednesday and Sunday, and the Luminous Mysteries on Thursday.

The Visitation

The Joyful Mysteries

1. **The Annunciation**
   Mary learns that she has been chosen to be the mother of Jesus.

2. **The Visitation**
   Mary visits Elizabeth, who tells her that she will always be remembered.

3. **The Nativity**
   Jesus is born in a stable in Bethlehem.

The Baptism of Jesus

4. **The Presentation**
   Mary and Joseph take the infant Jesus to the Temple to present him to God.

5. **The Finding of Jesus in the Temple**
   Jesus is found in the Temple, discussing his faith with the teachers.

The Mysteries of Light

The Crucifixion

1. **The Baptism of Jesus in the River Jordan**
   God proclaims that Jesus is his beloved Son.

2. **The Wedding Feast at Cana**
   At Mary's request Jesus performs his first miracle.

3. **The Proclamation of the Kingdom of God**
   Jesus calls all to conversion and service to the kingdom.

The Coming of the Holy Spirit

4. **The Transfiguration of Jesus**

   Jesus is revealed in glory to Peter, James, and John.

5. **The Institution of the Eucharist**

   Jesus offers his Body and Blood at the Last Supper.

The Sorrowful Mysteries

1. **The Agony in the Garden**

   Jesus prays in the Garden of Gethsemane on the night before he dies.

2. **The Scourging at the Pillar**

   Jesus is beaten with whips.

3. **The Crowning with Thorns**

   Jesus is mocked and crowned with thorns.

4. **The Carrying of the Cross**

   Jesus carries the cross on which he will be crucified.

5. **The Crucifixion**

   Jesus is nailed to the cross and dies.

The Glorious Mysteries

1. **The Resurrection**

   God the Father raises Jesus from the dead.

2. **The Ascension**

   Jesus returns to his Father in Heaven.

3. **The Coming of the Holy Spirit**

   The Holy Spirit comes to bring new life to the disciples.

4. **The Assumption of Mary**

   At the end of her life on earth, Mary is taken body and soul into Heaven.

5. **The Coronation of Mary**

   Mary is crowned as Queen of Heaven and Earth.

Stations of the Cross

The 14 Stations of the Cross represent events from Jesus' Passion and Death. At each station we use our senses and our imagination to reflect prayerfully on Jesus' suffering, Death, and Resurrection.

1

Jesus Is Condemned to Death.
Pontius Pilate condemns Jesus to death.

2

Jesus Takes Up the Cross.
Jesus willingly accepts and patiently bears the cross.

3

Jesus Falls the First Time.
Weakened by torments and loss of blood, Jesus falls beneath the cross.

4

Jesus Meets His Sorrowful Mother.
Jesus meets his mother, Mary, who is filled with grief.

5

Simon of Cyrene Helps Jesus Carry the Cross.
Soldiers force Simon of Cyrene to carry the cross.

6

Veronica Wipes the Face of Jesus.
Veronica steps through the crowd to wipe the face of Jesus.

7

Jesus Falls the Second Time.
Jesus falls beneath the weight of the cross a second time.

8

Jesus Meets the Women of Jerusalem.
Jesus tells the women not to weep for him, but for themselves and for their children.

9

Jesus Falls the Third Time.
Weakened almost to the point of death, Jesus falls a third time.

10

Jesus Is Stripped of His Garments.
The soldiers strip Jesus of his garments, treating him as a common criminal.

11

Jesus Is Nailed to the Cross.
Jesus' hands and feet are nailed to the cross.

12

Jesus Dies on the Cross.
After suffering greatly on the cross, Jesus bows his head and dies.

The closing prayer—sometimes included as a 15th station—reflects on the Resurrection of Jesus.

13

Jesus Is Taken Down from the Cross.
The lifeless body of Jesus is tenderly placed in the arms of Mary, his mother.

14

Jesus Is Laid in the Tomb.
Jesus' disciples place his body in the tomb.

Celebrating Our Faith

The Seven Sacraments

Jesus touches our lives through the sacraments. Our celebrations of the sacraments are signs of Christ's presence in our lives and a means for receiving his grace. The Church celebrates seven sacraments, which are divided into three categories.

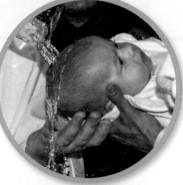

Sacraments of Initiation

These sacraments lay the foundation for our lives as Catholics.

Baptism

In Baptism we receive new life in Christ. Baptism takes away Original Sin and gives us a new birth in the Holy Spirit. Its sign is the pouring of water.

Confirmation

Confirmation seals our life of faith in Jesus. Its signs are the laying of hands on a person's head, most often by a bishop, and the anointing with oil. Like Baptism, Confirmation is received only once.

Eucharist

The Eucharist nourishes our life of faith. Its signs are the Bread and Wine we receive—the Body and Blood of Christ.

Sacraments of Healing

These sacraments celebrate the healing power of Jesus.

Penance and Reconciliation

Through Penance we receive God's forgiveness. Forgiveness requires being sorry for our sins. In Reconciliation we receive Jesus' healing grace through absolution by the priest. The signs of this sacrament are our confession of sins and the words of absolution.

Anointing of the Sick

This sacrament unites a sick person's suffering with that of Jesus and brings forgiveness of sins. Oil, a symbol of strength, is the sign of this sacrament. A person is anointed with oil and receives the laying on of hands from a priest.

Sacraments at the Service of Communion

These sacraments help members serve the community.

Holy Orders

In Holy Orders men are ordained as deacons, priests, or bishops. Deacons serve to remind us of our baptismal call to help others, and priests serve as spiritual leaders of their communities. Bishops carry on the teachings of the apostles. The signs of this sacrament are the laying on of hands and anointing with chrism by a bishop.

Matrimony

In Matrimony a baptized man and woman are united with each other as a sign of the unity between Jesus and his Church. Matrimony requires the consent of the couple, as expressed in the marriage promises. The couple and their wedding rings are the signs of this sacrament.

Celebrating the Lord's Day

Sunday is the day on which we celebrate the Resurrection of Jesus. Sunday is the Lord's Day. We gather for Mass, rest from work, and perform works of mercy. People all over the world gather at God's Eucharistic table as brothers and sisters.

The Order of Mass

The Mass is the most important sacramental celebration of the Church, and it always follows a set order.

Introductory Rites

We prepare to celebrate the Eucharist.

Entrance Chant

We gather as a community and praise God in song.

Greeting

We pray the Sign of the Cross. The priest welcomes us.

Penitential Act

We remember our sins and ask God for mercy.

Gloria

We praise God in song.

Collect

We ask God to hear our prayers.

Liturgy of the Word

We hear the story of God's plan for Salvation.

First Reading

We listen to God's Word, usually from the Old Testament.

Responsorial Psalm

We respond to God's Word in song.

Second Reading

We listen to God's Word from the New Testament.

Gospel Acclamation

We sing "Alleluia!" to praise God for the Good News. During Lent we use a different acclamation.

Gospel Reading

We stand and listen to the Gospel of the Lord.

Homily

The priest or the deacon explains God's Word.

Profession of Faith

We proclaim our faith through the Creed.

Prayer of the Faithful

We pray for our needs and the needs of others.

The four Gospel writers: Matthew, Mark, Luke, and John

Liturgy of the Eucharist

We celebrate Christ's presence in the Eucharist.

Presentation and Preparation of the Gifts

We bring gifts of bread and wine to the altar.

Prayer over the Offerings

The priest prays that God will accept our sacrifice.

Eucharistic Prayer

This prayer of thanksgiving is the center and high point of the entire celebration. The bread and wine are consecrated and become the Body and Blood of Jesus Christ.

▶ **Preface**—We give thanks and praise to God.

▶ **Holy, Holy, Holy**—We sing an acclamation of praise.

▶ **The Mystery of Faith**—We proclaim Jesus' Death and Resurrection.

▶ **Amen**—We affirm the words and actions of the Eucharistic Prayer.

Communion Rite

We prepare to receive the Body and Blood of Jesus Christ.

The Lord's Prayer

We pray the Lord's Prayer.

Sign of Peace

We offer one another Christ's peace.

Lamb of God

We pray for forgiveness, mercy, and peace.

Communion

We receive the Body and Blood of Jesus Christ.

Prayer after Communion

We pray that the Eucharist will strengthen us to live as Jesus did.

Concluding Rites

At the conclusion of Mass, we are blessed and sent forth.

Final Blessing

We receive God's blessing.

Dismissal

We go in peace to glorify the Lord by our lives.

Precepts of the Church

The Precepts of the Church describe the minimum effort we must make in prayer and in living a moral life. Catholics are called to move beyond the minimum by growing in love of God and love of neighbor. The Precepts are as follows:

1. attendance at Mass on Sundays and Holy Days of Obligation

2. confession of sin at least once a year

3. reception of Holy Communion at least once a year during the Easter season

4. observance of the days of fast and abstinence

5. providing for the needs of the Church

Holy Days of Obligation

Holy Days of Obligation are the days other than Sundays on which we celebrate the great things God has done for us through Jesus and the saints. On Holy Days of Obligation, Catholics attend Mass.

Six Holy Days of Obligation are celebrated in the United States.

January 1—Mary, Mother of God

40 days after Easter—Ascension

August 15—Assumption of the Blessed Virgin Mary

November 1—All Saints Day

December 8—Immaculate Conception

December 25—Nativity of Our Lord Jesus Christ

On November 1, we celebrate the lives of holy people such as Blessed Kateri Tekakwitha.

Antique glass icon of Jesus, Ukraine.

An Examination of Conscience

An examination of conscience is the act of looking prayerfully into our hearts to ask how we have hurt our relationships with God and other people through our thoughts, words, and actions. We reflect on the Ten Commandments and the teachings of the Church. Questions such as the following will help us in our examination of conscience.

My Relationship with God

What steps am I taking to help me grow closer to God and to others? Do I turn to God often during the day, especially when I am tempted?

Do I participate at Mass with attention and devotion on Sundays and holy days? Do I pray often and read the Bible?

Do I use God's name and the names of Jesus, Mary, and the saints with love and reverence?

My Relationships with Family, Friends, and Neighbors

Have I set a bad example through my words or actions? Do I treat others fairly? Do I spread stories that hurt other people?

Am I loving to those in my family? Am I respectful of my neighbors, my friends, and those in authority?

Do I show respect for my body and for the bodies of others? Do I keep away from forms of entertainment that do not respect God's gift of sexuality?

Have I taken or damaged anything that did not belong to me? Have I cheated, copied homework, or lied?

Do I quarrel with others just so I can get my own way? Do I insult others to try to make them think they are less than I am? Do I hold grudges and try to hurt people who I think have hurt me?

How to Go to Confession

An examination of conscience is an important part of preparing for the Sacrament of Penance and Reconciliation. The Sacrament of Reconciliation includes the following steps:

1. The priest greets us, and we pray the Sign of the Cross. He invites us to trust in God. He may read God's Word with us.

2. We confess our sins. The priest may help and counsel us.

3. The priest gives us a penance to perform. Penance is an act of kindness or prayers to pray, or both.

4. The priest asks us to express our sorrow, usually by reciting an Act of Contrition.

5. We receive absolution. The priest says, "I absolve you from your sins in the name of the Father, and of the Son, and of the Holy Spirit." We respond, "Amen."

6. The priest dismisses us by saying, "Go in peace." We go forth to perform the act of penance he has given us.

Making Good Choices

Our conscience is the inner voice that helps us to know the law God has placed in our hearts. Our conscience helps us to judge the moral qualities of our own actions. It guides us to do good and avoid evil.

The Holy Spirit can help us to form a good conscience. We form our conscience by studying the teachings of the Church and following the guidance of our parents and pastoral leaders.

The Seven Deadly Sins, Hieronymous Bosch.

Christian freedom upholds the dignity of every human being. It does not mean that we have the right to do whatever we please. We can live in true freedom if we cooperate with the Holy Spirit, who gives us the virtue of prudence. This virtue helps us to recognize what is good in every situation and to make correct choices. The Holy Spirit gives us the gifts of wisdom and understanding to help us make the right choices in life in relationship to God and others. The gift of counsel helps us to reflect on making correct choices in life.

The Ten Commandments help us to make moral choices that are pleasing to God. We have the grace of the sacraments, the teachings of the Church, and the good example of saints and fellow Christians to help us make good choices.

Making moral choices involves the following steps:

1. Ask the Holy Spirit for help.

2. Think about God's law and the teachings of the Church.

3. Think about what will happen as a result of your choice. Will the consequences be pleasing to God? Will your choice hurt someone else?

4. Seek advice from someone you respect and remember that Jesus is with you.

5. Ask yourself how your choice will affect your relationship with God and with others.

Making moral choices takes into consideration the object of the choice, our intention in making the choice, and the circumstances in which the choice is made. It is never right to make an evil choice in the hope of gaining something good.

Virtues

Virtues are gifts from God that lead us to live in a close relationship with him. Virtues are like habits. They need to be practiced; they can be lost if they are neglected. The three most important virtues are called Theological Virtues because they come from God and lead to God. The cardinal virtues are human virtues, acquired by education and good actions. *Cardinal* comes from the Latin word for *hinge (cardo)*, meaning "that on which other things depend."

Theological Virtues

faith	hope	charity

Cardinal Virtues

prudence	justice	fortitude	temperance

Gifts of the Holy Spirit

The Holy Spirit makes it possible for us to do what God asks of us by giving us these gifts.

wisdom	understanding	counsel
fortitude	knowledge	piety
fear of the Lord		

Fruits of the Holy Spirit

The Fruits of the Holy Spirit are signs of the Holy Spirit's action in our lives.

love	joy	peace
patience	kindness	generosity
faithfulness	gentleness	self-control

Church Tradition also includes goodness, modesty, and chastity as Fruits of the Holy Spirit.

Works of Mercy

The Corporal and Spiritual Works of Mercy are actions we can perform that extend God's compassion and mercy to those in need.

Corporal Works of Mercy

The Corporal Works of Mercy are kind acts by which we help our neighbors with their material and physical needs.

feed the hungry	shelter the homeless
clothe the naked	visit the sick and imprisoned
bury the dead	give alms to the poor

Spiritual Works of Mercy

The Spiritual Works of Mercy are acts of compassion by which we help our neighbors with their emotional and spiritual needs.

instruct	advise
console	comfort
forgive	bear wrongs patiently

Showing Our Love for the World

In the story of the Good Samaritan (Luke 10:29–37), Jesus makes clear our responsibility to care for those in need. The Catholic Church teaches this responsibility in the following themes of Catholic Social Teaching.

Life and Dignity of the Human Person

All human life is sacred, and all people must be respected and valued over material goods. We are called to ask whether our actions as a society respect or threaten the life and dignity of the human person.

Call to Family, Community, and Participation

Participation in family and community is central to our faith and to a healthy society. Families must be supported so that people can participate in society, build a community spirit, and promote the well-being of all, especially those who are poor and vulnerable.

Rights and Responsibilities

Every person has a right to life as well as a right to those things required for human decency. As Catholics we have a responsibility to protect these basic human rights in order to achieve a healthy society.

Option for the Poor and Vulnerable

In our world many people are very rich while at the same time many are extremely poor. As Catholics we are called to pay special attention to the needs of those who are poor by defending and promoting their dignity and by meeting their immediate material needs.

The Dignity of Work and the Rights of Workers

The basic rights of workers must be respected: the right to productive work, fair wages, and private property; and the right to organize, join unions, and pursue economic opportunity. Catholics believe that the economy is meant to serve people and that work is not merely a way to make a living but is an important way in which we participate in God's creation.

Solidarity

Because God is our Father, we are all brothers and sisters with the responsibility to care for one another. Solidarity is the attitude that leads Christians to share spiritual and material goods. Solidarity unites rich and poor, weak and strong, and helps to make a society that recognizes that we all depend upon one another.

Care for God's Creation

God is the Creator of all people and all things, and he wants us to enjoy his creation. The responsibility to care for all God has made is a requirement of our faith.

Songs of Our Faith

Song of Love

Chorus

Thank you, Jesus, for helping me to see.
Thank you, God, for the heart you've given me.
Thank you, Spirit, for coming to me,
and for showing me how to sing your song of love.

Verse 1

I saw someone lonely by the road,
someone my age sadly all alone.
I shared my friendship, and we talked a while.
I gave my hand. Jesus gave back a smile.

(Sing Chorus)

Verse 2

I saw Jesus inside my heart,
making me God's own work of art.
If I spread my joy in life each day,
I can show my love for God's world
    in every way.

Verse 3

I saw Jesus in friends and family
by my side, sharing and supporting me.
I found my heart had room for everyone.
Thank you, Spirit, for what you have begun.

(Sing Chorus)

Lyrics by E. Strauss. Music by Neilson Hubbard.
© 2005 Loyola Press. All rights reserved.

Sing Out, Earth and Skies

Verse 1

Come, O God of all the earth:
Come to us, O Righteous One;
Come, and bring our love to birth:
In the glory of your Son.

Refrain

Sing out, earth and skies!
Sing of the God who loves you!
Raise your joyful cries!
Dance to the life around you!

Verse 2

Come, O God of wind and flame:
Fill the earth with righteousness;
Teach us all to sing your name:
May our lives your love confess.

(Sing Refrain)

Verse 3

Come, O God of flashing light:
Twinkling star and burning sun;
God of day and God of night:
In your light we all are one.

(Sing Refrain)

Verse 4

Come, O God of snow and rain:
Shower down upon the earth;
Come, O God of joy and pain:
God of sorrow, God of mirth.

(Sing Refrain)

Verse 5

Come, O Justice, Come, O Peace:
Come and shape our hearts anew;
Come and make oppression cease:
Bring us all to life in you.

(Sing Refrain)

Let the Children Come to Me

Refrain

"Let the children come to me;
let the children come.
Never hinder them; never stop them.
O let the children come."

Verse 1

People were bringing children,
just to see the Lord.
And when the disciples stopped them,
This is what they heard:

(Sing Refrain)

Verse 2

"If you seek the kingdom,
listen to what I say:
Unless you become like children,
you cannot know the way."

(Sing Refrain)

Verse 3

Then the Lord embraced them,
held them in his care.
With love he bestowed his blessing,
with love he spoke this prayer:

(Sing Refrain)

When Jesus the Healer

Verse 1

When Jesus the healer passed through Galilee,
Heal us, heal us today.
The deaf came to hear and the blind came to see.
Heal us, Lord Jesus.

Verse 2

A paralyzed man was let down through a roof.
Heal us, heal us today.
His sins were forgiven, his walking the proof.
Heal us, Lord Jesus.

Verse 3

The death of his daughter caused Jairus to weep.
Heal us, heal us today.
The Lord took her hand, and he raised her from sleep.
Heal us, Lord Jesus.

Verse 4

When blind Bartimaeus cried out to the Lord,
Heal us, heal us today.
His faith made him whole and his sight was restored.
Heal us, Lord Jesus.

Verse 5

The lepers were healed and the demons cast out.
Heal us, heal us today.
A bent woman straightened to laugh and to shout.
Heal us, Lord Jesus.

"When Jesus the Healer" words and music by Peter D. Smith.
Words and music © 1978 Stainer & Bell Ltd. and Methodist Church (UK),
Division of Education and Youth. Administered by Hope Publishing Co.,
Carol Stream, IL 60188. All rights reserved. Used by permission.

Immaculate Mary

Verse 1

Immaculate Mary, your praises we sing;
You reign now in splendor with Jesus our King.

Refrain

Ave, Ave, Ave Maria.
Ave, Ave, Ave Maria.

Verse 2

To you by an angel, the Lord God made known
The grace of the Spirit, the gift of the Son.

(Sing Refrain)

Verse 3

The angels rejoiced when you brought forth God's Son;
Your joy is the joy of all ages to come.

(Sing Refrain)

Verse 4

Your child is the Savior, all hope lies in him:
He gives us new life and redeems us from sin.

(Sing Refrain)

Verse 5

In glory forever now close to your Son,
All ages will praise you for all God has done.

(Sing Refrain)

*"Immaculate Mary" by Brian Foley. © 1971 Faber Music Ltd.
Reproduced by kind permission of the publishers.*

Jesus, Bread of Life

Refrain

Jesus, Jesus: Bread of Life.
Jesus, Jesus: saving cup.
Jesus, Jesus, live in us.
We believe, O God, we believe.

Verse 1

"I am the bread which comes from heaven.
Those who eat will never die."

(Sing Refrain)

Verse 2

"Come now to me, all who are thirsty.
Come and drink with faith in me."

(Sing Refrain)

Verse 3

"Be not afraid; do not be troubled.
Trust in God and trust in me."

(Sing Refrain)

Verse 4

"Abide in me; keep my commandments.
Learn to love as I have loved you."

(Sing Refrain)

Make Me a Channel of Your Peace

Verse 1

Make me a channel of your peace.
Where there is hatred, let me bring your love.
Where there is injury, your pardon, Lord,
And where there's doubt, true faith in you.

Verse 2

Make me a channel of your peace,
Where there's despair in life, let me bring hope.
Where there is darkness, only light,
And where there's sadness, ever joy.

Verse 3

Oh Master, grant that I may never seek
So much to be consoled as to console.
To be understood as to understand.
To be loved as to love with all my soul.

Verse 4

Make me a channel of your peace.
It is in pardoning that we are pardoned,
in giving of ourselves that we receive,
and in dying that we're born to eternal life.

Prayer of Peace

Verse 1

Peace before us, peace behind us,
peace under our feet.
Peace within us, peace over us,
let all around us be peace.

Verse 2

Love before us, love behind us,
love under our feet.
Love within us, love over us,
let all around us be love.

Verse 3

Light before us, light behind us,
light under our feet.
Light within us, light over us,
let all around us be light.

Verse 4

Christ before us, Christ behind us,
Christ under our feet.
Christ within us, Christ over us,
let all around us be Christ.

Name _____ Date _____

Art Print 1 shows a woman preparing lilies to be used as an offering to God. What are some ways you can show God you are thankful for his creations?

God Creates the World

God made the world because he was inspired to do so. Creation came from God's love, and it continues to be a manifestation of God's love.

God cares for the world and everything in it equally. The lowly inchworm is as much a creation of God as the massive whale. We are living as God wants us to when we respect every one of his creations.

God Continues to Care for the World

God put his love and care into his creation. When each of the planet's small but important aspects was rendered, God looked upon it and was pleased by it.

Although God holds us and all his creatures in his safekeeping, he counts on us to be the custodians on earth. That means caring daily for one another and for all creatures, great and small. We have the responsibility to love and care for the world that God so lovingly created. By caring for God's creations, we show God that we, in turn, care for him.

Taking the Pledge

Make a list of some of your favorites of God's creation. _____

_____

_____

I will show God that I love and care for these things by _____

_____

_____.

Link to Liturgy

The Preface, which recalls God's work in creation, begins the Eucharistic Prayer.

Name _____ Date _____

Art Print 2 shows Saint Peter Claver, who helped the enslaved people of South America and preached against injustice. What do you do when you witness an injustice?

Saint Peter Claver, the "Saint of Slaves"

Saint Peter Claver devoted his life to helping slaves. He was born in Spain in 1581, but he spent most of his life in South America as a missionary to slaves.

Peter Claver gave the slaves physical and spiritual care from the moment they arrived from Africa. He met them at the harbor with food and medicine. He tried to persuade their masters to treat them humanely. He also comforted the slaves and taught them about Jesus, encouraging them to live as Christians. By 1615 Peter Claver is said to have baptized more than 300,000 slaves. He died in 1654. His feast day is September 9.

Our Humanity

As humans we are capable of both good and harmful actions. When we sin, we say no to what God wants of us. When we confess our sins, we are forgiven and are able to start anew. Each day is an opportunity to do our best, to be courageous, to defend those who are weak, and to be more like Jesus.

Consider a way in which you would like to improve upon your Christianity. On the lines below, write a goal for tomorrow to be more like Jesus. Think of why it is important for you to achieve this goal.

_____

_____

_____

_____

_____

_____

Name _____ Date _____

Art Print 3 shows Moses with the tablets containing the Ten Commandments. Why do you think God gave us the Ten Commandments?

God's Word

The inspired testimony of God's Word is recorded in the Bible. Among the Bible's important stories and lessons, the Ten Commandments stand out as the most important and comprehensive of God's hopes for his people. God gave them to Moses, who passed them on to the Israelites, and to us. The Ten Commandments are tools for living peaceful and loving lives.

Finding Bible Passages

Bible passages are identified by book, chapter, and verse.

The story of Creation begins in Genesis. Genesis is the first book of the Bible. The number before the colon identifies the chapter, and the number or series of numbers after the colon identifies the verse or verses.

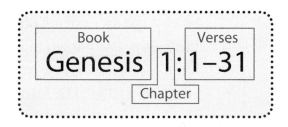

Find the following Scripture passages and answer the questions.

1. **Exodus 3:1–4**   How did God appear to Moses?

   _____

   _____

2. **Exodus 3:7–8**   What did God say he will do for his people?

   _____

   _____

3. **Exodus 3:10**   What did God ask Moses to do?

   _____

   _____

Name _____   Date _____

Art Print 4 shows Saint Philip Neri listening to the confession of Pope Clement VIII.
What are some talents you have that you can use to help others?

Saint Philip Neri, the Saint of Joy and Humility

Philip Neri, born in 1515 in Florence, Italy, was a down-to-earth man who taught that being holy does not mean being serious all the time. He loved a good joke. In fact, his favorite books were the New Testament and a joke book. When he taught young people about their faith, he told them, "Be good—if you can."

Philip himself achieved a great deal of good. He moved to Rome and cared for people who were sick and poor. Then Philip became a priest. He encouraged people to be humble and to receive the sacraments often to be close to Jesus. Philip was also known to encourage happiness, often saying, "Worrywarts and long faces, stay away from here." His feast day is May 26.

Following the Example

Saint Philip Neri taught people to be closer to God by being good and happy. How can you serve God's kingdom? List three ways.

_____

_____

_____

? Did You Know?

In his life and community, Saint Philip Neri lived out one form of Christian spirituality. Saints like Ignatius of Loyola, Francis of Assisi, and Dominic formed their own communities to live out Christian spirituality in distinct and diverse ways.

Name _____ Date _____

Art Print 5 shows a woman surrounded by symbols and objects that give her peace.
What are some things that bring you peace in your life?

Celebrating Ordinary Time

We enjoy holidays and special days because we anticipate the joy and attention of our families, friends, and communities as they share our excitement.

While we look forward to holidays and celebrations, there are joyful events happening every day of the year. Each ordinary day that we wake up to God's love is a day to see our blessings and be thankful.

We Celebrate God

Ordinary Time celebrates the everyday relationship we share with God and our community. During Ordinary Time we celebrate the gift of the sacraments. They serve as special opportunities of grace to enhance our relationship with God. We use sacramentals, such as rituals and sacred oils, to stay connected with God every day.

Ordinary Joy

"This is the day the LORD has made;
let us rejoice in it and be glad."

Psalm 118:24

Think about the message of Psalm 118. On the lines below, write a few things that you are thankful for that make you glad in your everyday life.

_____

_____

_____

_____

_____

_____

Name _____ Date _____

Art Print 6 shows Jesus teaching his disciples that they are the building blocks of the Church. In what ways are you a building block in your family or at school?

Jesus'—and Our—Role in the Church

The New Testament uses a special image to show the Church's nature.

> So then you are no longer strangers and sojourners, but you are . . . members of the household of God, built upon the foundation of the apostles and the prophets, with Christ Jesus himself as the capstone. Through him the whole structure is held together and grows into a temple sacred in the Lord; in him you . . . are being built together into a dwelling place of God in the Spirit.
>
> *Ephesians 2:19–22*

This passage compares the Church to a temple of living stones. In this temple, Jesus is like a capstone, the crowning point of a building. The followers, like us, are the cornerstones, the foundation of the building. Without cornerstones the building could not stand. This shows the unity between Jesus and the Church. The Church lives from, in, and for Jesus; Jesus lives with the Church and in the Church.

The cornerstone, or foundation stone, determines the position of the entire structure.

As followers of Jesus, we are like stones in the temple that is the Church. We are the living sign of God's presence in the world. As believers we have an important role in the Church.

Building Your Life

On a separate sheet of paper, make a "building" of your life, with you as the cornerstone. Show whom you depend on and the people who depend on you. Notice where Jesus fits on your building.

Reading God's Word

Therefore, thus says the Lord GOD:
    See, I am laying a stone in Zion,
    a stone that has been tested,
A precious cornerstone as a sure foundation;
    he who puts his faith in it shall not be shaken.

Isaiah 28:16

Name _____ Date _____

Art Print 7 shows a group of people at the bedside of Jairus's ill daughter. When we are scared or worried, we often turn to God to ask for help. Why do you think we find comfort in praying to God in difficult times?

Jesus Heals Jairus's Daughter

Jesus was preaching to a crowd when Jairus arrived and fell at his feet. Jairus said, "My daughter is dying. Please, lay your hands on her that she may live."

Jesus went. On the way people from Jairus's house met them and said, "Your daughter has died." Jesus said, "Be not afraid. Have faith." Jairus trusted Jesus and proceeded home. There his family was weeping. Jesus said, "Why are you crying? The child is not dead but asleep."

Jesus took her hand, saying, "Arise." The girl stood before her astonished parents.

adapted from Mark 5:21–24,35–42

Christ's Presence in the Sacraments

The raising of Jairus's daughter shows God's healing power through Jesus' touch and words. Jesus touches our lives today through the sacraments. The words proclaim the meaning of the celebration. The physical objects—water, Bread and Wine, oil, and hands of blessing—are the signs of Jesus touching our lives. The sacraments call us to give witness to Jesus Christ's presence in the world.

Letter from Jairus's Daughter

Imagine you received a letter from Jairus's daughter, explaining how it felt to be healed by Jesus. How would she have described the experience? On a separate sheet of paper, write what you think the letter would say.

Reading God's Word

Jesus did this . . . and so revealed his glory, and his disciples began to believe in him.

John 2:11

Name _____ Date _____

Art Print 8 shows Peter preaching with Mark to a crowd. If you had a crowd listening to you, what passion of yours would you want to discuss?

Peter Calls for Repentance and Baptism

After Jesus ascended into Heaven, the disciples heard a strong wind as the Spirit came upon them. People gathered to listen and heard the disciples speaking. Peter told the story of Jesus' life, Death, and Resurrection. He said that Jesus was God's Chosen One, the Savior.

Moved by the story, the crowd asked, "What do we do?"

Peter answered, "Repent and be baptized. Your sins will be forgiven, and you will receive the Holy Spirit."

adapted from Acts of the Apostles 2:1–13,22–38

Jesus, Salvation, and the Sacraments of Initiation

Peter stated basic Christian beliefs: Jesus died on the cross for our Salvation. Peter's sermon ends in hope: If we repent and accept Jesus in Baptism and Confirmation, we will receive the Holy Spirit. Through the Sacraments of Initiation—Baptism, Confirmation, and the Eucharist—we are brought into the fullness of the Spirit as we become members of the Church.

Interviewing Saint Peter

Imagine you have the opportunity to interview Saint Peter. On a separate sheet of paper, write the questions you would like to ask him about repentance and Salvation. Think about what his answers might be.

Meet a Saint

Saint Francis Xavier was one of the first Jesuits. He worked in India and Japan, preaching the word of Jesus to people who were impoverished. He gave up his worldy goods and comforts to share God's Word. Francis told many people about Jesus' call to a new life, and many answered the call. As a missionary he baptized more than 40,000 people. His feast day is December 3.

Name _____   Date _____

Art Print 9 shows disciples joyfully receiving the Holy Spirit.
When was a time you felt the Holy Spirit?

Given a Mission

After Jesus' Ascension into Heaven, the apostles' mission was to spread the news of Salvation and act as witnesses to Jesus. The Holy Spirit came to aid them in their mission when the apostles, Mary, and the other disciples were gathered during the Jewish feast of Pentecost, which marked the time when God gave the Ten Commandments to Moses.

> And suddenly there came from the sky a noise like a strong, driving wind. There appeared to them tongues of fire, which came to rest on each of them. They were filled with the Holy Spirit and began to speak in different tongues, as the Spirit enabled them to proclaim.
>
> *adapted from Acts of the Apostles 2:2–4*

The Holy Spirit moved the apostles to proclaim the good news about Jesus and the new Covenant that fulfills the promise God made to Abraham.

Wind is a symbol of God's action in the story of Salvation. The Holy Spirit also came as tongues of fire. The symbolism of fire goes back to when God gave Moses the Ten Commandments and smoke rose from the mountain as if it were on fire. At Pentecost the fire again shows God acting in the world.

Acting Out Our Mission

Like the apostles, we have a mission to proclaim the good news of Salvation. What is one way we act out our mission?

_____

_____

_____

Name _____ Date _____

*Art Print 10 shows a family walking in the snow to attend Christmas Eve Mass.
What emotions do you feel during Advent? What do you do to get ready for Jesus?*

Celebrating Advent

Advent is the season that begins four Sundays
before Christmas during which the Church
prepares to celebrate the coming of Jesus
Christ. The period of four weeks
reminds us of the centuries in which
the People of Israel, God's chosen
people, waited for the Messiah.
Advent also celebrates the Feast of
the Immaculate Conception, which
honors Mary's conception without
Original Sin.

In anticipation of Christmas, we get ready by preparing with the sacraments.
We turn away from sin and live more attentively to the ways of God by
participating in the Sacrament of Reconciliation. We recall the gift of our
Baptism, the sacrament that makes us members of God's family. We receive
the Eucharist, which reminds us of the Life, Death, and Resurrection of Jesus
and God's gift of eternal life.

Preparing with My Family

Although we "celebrate" the season of Advent, the season is a time of preparation.
Think of all the ways you and your family prepare during Advent, such as going
to Mass together. What special traditions or things do you do together to ready
yourselves for Jesus' coming? On the lines below, write one way your family
prepares for Jesus and one new tradition you can introduce to your family this year.

_____

_____

_____

_____

Name _____ Date _____

Art Print 11 shows a community praising God together. What is one way you can help your Church community?

Unity and Diversity in the Church

Individually we are called to use our different gifts to serve our community. The Church is called the Body of Christ because Jesus is one with his Church. We share this unity as a Church family. The Church is both unified and diverse. Saint Paul explains this.

> Just as a body has many parts but is still one body, so it is with Jesus Christ. No matter what your nationality, we are all one, because we are all baptized by the Holy Spirit into the same body, the Church.
>
> *adapted from 1 Corinthians 12:12–13*

Paul emphasizes that we are joined to one another, and God, in the Church, by the Holy Spirit. This unity is made possible by the gift of God's grace.

Paul also recognizes the diversity in the Church. Church members come from many different cultures and speak many different languages. They possess a variety of gifts from the Holy Spirit and are called to use those gifts in many different ways.

In My Parish...

Think about your own parish. How is diversity and unity reflected?

_____

_____

_____

Did You Know?

The liturgy is celebrated in many languages, including the Native American languages of Navajo and Choctaw.

© LOYOLAPRESS.

Name _____ Date _____

Art Print 12 shows Pope John Paul II meeting with the bishops to reaffirm the Church's message. Through the Sacrament of Holy Orders, men are called to be leaders in the Church. Why is this mission of the Church leaders so important?

The Apostles Choose a New Member

Jesus chose 12 men to be apostles. One of them, Judas, betrayed Jesus and then punished himself for betraying Jesus. After Jesus' Ascension, the apostles had the important mission of spreading the news about Jesus. But they were lacking one member. Here is how the apostles chose a replacement.

> Peter informed a large group of Jesus' followers that a replacement for Judas was needed. He explained that this person needed to have been a witness to Jesus' life, Death, and Resurrection. Two people were proposed, Justus and Matthias. Peter and the apostles prayed for the Lord to show them whom to choose. Matthias was chosen; he became the new apostle.
>
> *adapted from Acts of the Apostles 1:15–26*

The disciples chose a new Church leader to be a witness to Jesus Christ and continue his work. Today the pope, bishops, and priests have been chosen to continue Jesus' work; they are the successors of the apostles.

Letter to Clergy

On a separate sheet of paper, write a letter to your parish priest or deacon, thanking him for guiding the Church's mission.

Reading God's Word

And so I say to you, you are Peter, and upon this rock I will build my church, and the gates of the netherworld shall not prevail against it.

Matthew 16:18

Name _____ Date _____

Art Print 13 shows Mary finding Jesus in the Temple after worrying about his disappearance. Think of a time in your life when you did not respect your family's rules. How could you handle it better in the future?

Jesus in the Temple as a Child

Jesus grew up in a family with his parents, Mary and Joseph. His family was faithful to the traditions of Judaism, observing the feasts and praying together. The Gospel of Luke tells how the 12-year-old Jesus remained in Jerusalem after the festival of Passover.

When the festival days had ended, Mary and Joseph began their return journey to Nazareth, unaware Jesus was not with them. When they discovered he was not among the caravan, they returned to Jerusalem. After searching for Jesus for three days, they found him in the Temple, speaking with and listening to the teachers, who were impressed with Jesus' wisdom and understanding.

When Joseph and Mary saw Jesus, Mary asked him why he had done this and worried them so. Jesus replied, "Why were you looking for me? Did you not know that I must be in my Father's house?" His parents were astonished.

Jesus returned to Nazareth with his parents and was obedient to them. He grew up in Nazareth, gradually gaining understanding and wisdom.

adapted from Luke 2:42–52

Lost and Found

On a separate sheet of paper, write about a time you were lost or separated from your group or family. How did you feel to be found again?

Sacred Site

The original Temple in Jerusalem housed the Ark of the Covenant, which contained the Ten Commandments. Before Jesus' time the Temple had been destroyed and rebuilt. It was destroyed for the last time by Romans in A.D. 70.

Name _____ Date _____

Art Print 14 shows Joseph working together with Jesus, using their skills to answer God's call. How do you use your talents to serve God?

The Universal Call to Holiness

In 1988 Pope John Paul II wrote about the vocation to holiness as something every person is called to. Because the Spirit is in us, we are all called to live holy lives within such areas as politics, mass media, economics, science, and the arts. In their vocation as laypeople, single or married, the laity seek the Kingdom of God by following the Gospel everyday.

Assembling a Sculpture

On November 4, 1999, Cardinal James Hickey, the archbishop of Washington, D.C., led the dedication for the sculpture *Universal Call to Holiness*. This work was made by the American sculptor George Carr. First, Carr designed a small model for approval. Then Carr made a full-scale clay model.

This large model was sent to Tuscany, Italy, where 22 skilled sculptors used it to carve the design out of huge slabs of marble. The slabs were then transported to the United States, where architect Anthony Segreti and construction consultants put the huge pieces into place. Workers moved the pieces with hand-operated pulleys since the abrupt on-and-off thrusts caused by electric pulleys could have damaged the pieces. The work was possible because of the cooperation of people with diverse backgrounds and skills.

Cooperating on a Project

Have you ever worked as part of a team or on a group project? What talents did you share? How did the project turn out? Choose one experience, and write on a separate sheet of paper a few sentences about that experience.

Name _____ Date _____

Art Print 15 shows a Nativity scene celebrating the night Jesus was born. What do you do to celebrate Jesus' coming?

Celebrating Christmas

Our celebration of Christmas begins on Christmas Eve and ends on the Feast of the Baptism of the Lord. During the Christmas season, we celebrate Jesus' birth, his manifestation to the world, and his baptism. The Feast of the Epiphany marks the day that Jesus was visited by the Magi, who had spent nearly a year crossing the Syrian Desert to worship him. Their journey to see Jesus illustrated that his birth would change the world for all people everywhere.

The word *epiphany* means a new understanding. Jesus' presence among us changed the way people thought and lived. The practice of Christianity was set in motion and spread around the world.

The Gift of Jesus

Although the celebration of Christmas comes with lights and presents and parties, its most important element is the new understanding that comes with it. Jesus taught us to take care of one another, to forgive one another, and to make God more important than any earthly desire.

> One of the scribes, when he came forward and heard them disputing and saw how well [Jesus] had answered them, asked him, "Which is the first of all the commandments?" Jesus replied, "The first is this: 'Hear, O Israel! The Lord our God is Lord alone! You shall love the Lord your God with all your heart, with all your soul, with all your mind, and with all your strength.' The second is this: 'You shall love your neighbor as yourself.' There is no other commandment greater than these."
>
> *Mark 12:28–31*

Show Your Love

Write one way you can show your love for God and one way you can show your love toward others.

_____

_____

Name _____ Date _____

Art Print 16 shows Jesus and his disciples feeding Jesus' followers.
Who or what in your life provides you nourishment?

Jesus Feeds the Crowd

One day Jesus was preaching to a crowd, and mealtime was nearing. He asked his disciple Philip where they could buy food for the nearly 5,000 gathered. Philip answered, "Two hundred days' wages could not feed each person even a little."

Andrew said, "A boy in the crowd has five barley loaves and two fish, but what good are these for so many?" Jesus took the loaves and fishes, gave thanks, and gave them to the crowd. All assembled ate their fill. When the people saw what Jesus had done, they said, "This is truly the Prophet." They wanted to make him king.

Jesus said to them, "I am the bread of life; whoever comes to me will never hunger, and whoever believes in me will never thirst."

adapted from John 6:1–15;34–35

Jesus, the Bread of Life

The people in the story didn't fully understand Jesus' mission. They ask Jesus if he is like Moses, who fed the Hebrews in the desert. That bread was called manna, and it fell daily from Heaven for the freed slaves to eat.

Like manna, Jesus nourishes for all eternity those who believe. Jesus says that he is the living Bread who came from Heaven and that whoever eats this Bread will have everlasting life in Heaven. He is referring to the Eucharist, which he was to institute at the Last Supper.

Nourished by Faith

Write an example of how your faith in Jesus has helped or nourished you through a difficult time.

_____

_____

_____

Art Print 20 shows a close-up of Jesus as he carries his cross, though he does not condemn his persecutors. Has there been a time when you had to forgive someone or ask for forgiveness? How did it feel?

Jesus Forgives

The week Jesus died began with his triumphal entry into Jerusalem on Palm Sunday as the people cried out, "Blessed is the king who comes in the name of the Lord." Later in the week Jesus shared a final meal with his disciples on Holy Thursday. That evening he was arrested. The next morning, Good Friday, Jesus came before Pilate.

When Jesus stood before Pilate to be judged, the crowd turned against Jesus and shouted for his crucifixion. Pilate told the crowd that Jesus had done nothing wrong. The crowd demanded the release of Barabbas, a criminal and murderer. Pilate did as the crowd asked. He released Barabbas and condemned Jesus.

Jesus carried his cross to the hill where he was crucified next to two other criminals, one on his right, the other on his left. Before he died Jesus said, "Father, forgive them, they know not what they do."

adapted from Luke 23:1–25,33–43

Forgive as Jesus Did

Sometimes words can become so familiar to us that we don't think about what we are saying. In the Lord's Prayer, look again at the words "forgive us our trespasses, as we forgive those who trespass against us." Now that you have read the story of the Crucifixion, think about what these words mean to you.

Celebrating Lent and Holy Week

The Lenten season is our opportunity to follow Jesus' example in our lives to prepare for Easter. We rededicate ourselves to resist temptation, practice almsgiving, and abstain from meat on Fridays. Making a promise to God and yourself to do something positive or giving toward others is also encouraged.

Write two ways you can celebrate the Lenten season. Choose things that would remind you, daily, of Christ's strength when tempted and his ultimate sacrifice.

_____

_____

Art Print 17 shows Jesus and his disciples sharing in the Last Supper. Why is sharing a meal important to you and your family?

The Eucharist Calls Us to Share

An ordained priest leads the celebration of the Eucharist. Jesus Christ is present through the priest. The Eucharistic liturgy remembers the sacrifice Jesus made for us. We participate by receiving the Eucharist, a **memorial,** or remembrance, of this sacrifice, which redeems our sins and offers us everlasting life.

According to Saint Paul, Christians cannot truly celebrate the Eucharist unless they are ready to love and share with one another. Paul was especially critical of those who were rich, who would gather with the community to eat but not to share what they had.

> Therefore, whoever eats the bread or drinks the cup of the Lord unworthily will have to answer for the body and blood of the Lord. A person should examine himself, and so eat the bread and drink the cup. For anyone who eats and drinks without discerning the body, eats and drinks judgment on him. *adapted from 1 Corinthians 11:27–29*

By "discerning the body," Paul means that those celebrating the Eucharist must understand that Jesus died for many people. To receive the Body and the Blood of Christ "worthily," we should be ready to live like Jesus.

Worthy of the Eucharist

On a separate sheet of paper, write ways in which you can act worthy of receiving the Eucharist.

Reading God's Word

Therefore, if you bring your gift to the altar, and there recall that your brother has anything against you, leave your gift there at the altar, go first and be reconciled with your brother, and then come and offer your gift.

Matthew 5:23–24

Art Print 18 shows Jesus revealing himself to his apostles after he is risen. Think of a time when you were at your lowest and you asked Jesus for help. How did you feel?

Jesus Brings Us Peace and Forgiveness

The apostles were gathered together after Jesus died, afraid of what the authorities might do to them as Jesus' followers.

On the evening of the first day of the week, when the doors were locked where the disciples were, Jesus appeared and said to them, "Peace be with you." He showed them his hands and his side. The disciples rejoiced when they saw the Lord. Jesus said to them again, "Peace be with you. As the Father has sent me, so I send you." Then, he breathed on them and said to them, "Receive the Holy Spirit. Whose sins you forgive are forgiven them, and whose sins you retain, are retained."

adapted from John 20:19–23

The risen Jesus brings peace. This gift of the Holy Spirit helps people live in harmony with others and with themselves. This is reconciliation, the returning of harmony to our broken relationships with God, with others, and even with ourselves. In the Gospel story, Jesus gives the apostles the authority to forgive sins and reconcile people with God and with one another. The Church celebrates that gift in the Sacrament of Reconciliation.

Learning to Forgive

Think about a time when you asked for forgiveness from someone whom you wronged. Then recall a time when someone asked for your forgiveness. Write a brief prayer to God, thanking him for the strength to forgive and to be forgiven yourself.

_____

_____

_____

_____

_____

Art Print 19 shows Peter and John healing a man who was crippled, w... with God's work. When was a time you thanked God for something gr...

The Apostles Heal in Jesus' Name

Now Peter and John were going up to the temple area for the three o'clo... prayer. And a man crippled from birth was carried and placed at the gate... called "the Beautiful Gate" every day to beg for alms from the people who e... temple. When he saw Peter and John about to go into the temple, he asked... But Peter looked intently at him, as did John, and said, "Look at us." He paid a... to them, expecting to receive something from them. Peter said, "I have neither... gold, but what I do have I give you: in the name of Jesus Christ the Nazorean, [r... walk." Then Peter took him by the right hand and raised him up, and immediately... feet and ankles grew strong. He leaped up, stood, and walked around, and went int... temple with them, walking and jumping and praising God. When all the people saw... walking and praising God, they recognized him as the one who used to sit begging at... the Beautiful Gate of the temple, and they were filled with amazement and astonishment... of what had happened to him.

Acts of the Apostles 3:1–1...

The healed man's response to God's act was overwhelming joy, expressed in an outpouring of praise to God. God continues to heal in the Church through the Holy Spirit. By uniting our prayers with Jesus in the Spirit, God will always hear us and answer in some way.

Gratitude List

On a separate sheet of paper, list five things in your life that make you happy. Write a brief prayer to God, giving thanks for all he has done for you.

Link to Liturgy

Before we receive Holy Communion, we acknowledge our dependence on God. We pray, "Lord, I am not worthy that you should enter under my roof, but only say the word and my soul shall be healed."

Name _____ Date _____

Art Print 21 shows Saint Francis of Assisi surrounded by birds, God's creations.
What in nature inspires you?

Saint Francis of Assisi

As a young man in the Italian town of
Assisi, Francis (1181–1226), the son of a
silk merchant, liked to go to parties and
have fun with friends. He wanted to be a
knight but was captured during a battle
and held as a prisoner for ransom.

After his release from prison, Francis
returned to Assisi but no longer felt he
fit in. He began to notice people who
were poor and sick, and he began to
help them. One night in a dream, he
received a call from Jesus to help rebuild
his Church. Francis thought Jesus meant
the small, rundown chapel at the edge
of town. So he sold some goods from his father's shop to pay for the rebuilding.
His father, very angry at Francis's action, disowned him. Francis gave back all
his possessions to his father—even his clothing, and from then on wore only a
brown cloak belted with a rope.

Francis dedicated his life to God and to the care of poor people. Although some
people made fun of him for wearing such humble clothes and sharing the company
of people who were sick and poor, Francis was happy and even danced with joy.

Eventually many others followed him, and he became the center of a community
dedicated to helping others. Francis's simple brown cloak became the **habit**, or
uniform, of his community of followers.

Francis's message taught many to see God's love, not material objects, as most
important and fulfilling. His feast day is October 4.

Everyday Appreciation

On a separate sheet of paper, write how you can live the message of Saint Francis
in your everyday life.

Name _____   Date _____

Art Print 22 shows three women sharing gossip as they go about their day.
Why do you think spreading and listening to gossip is so harmful?

Words Out of Control

This Jewish folktale discusses the effects of gossip.

One day a man went to his rabbi to ask for help. The man found out
that people were falsely saying he was overcharging customers in his shop.

The rabbi discovered that a woman of the town had started the rumor.
He told her that he believed she was spreading an untrue story. The woman
felt bad, and she said she would tell everyone that her story was not true.

The rabbi thought for a moment, then said, "First, get a pillow and go to
the top of a hill and let out all the feathers. Then pick up the feathers and
bring them back to me. Be sure to get them all."

The woman did as she was told. The wind got hold of the feathers, and the
air was soon full of feathers going in all directions. The woman tried, but she
realized that she could never catch them all.

The woman told the rabbi what had happened. He replied that just as it was
impossible to retrieve all the feathers, it is impossible to find all who had heard
the false story about the shopkeeper. He encouraged her to do what she could
to remedy the situation. So the woman went to shop at the man's store every
day and praised the goods she bought there.

Words Can Hurt

Write a brief poem that shows how harmful words and gossip can be to others.

_____

_____

_____

_____

Name _____ Date _____

Art Print 23 shows Kateri Tekakwitha surrounded by different symbols of her faith and culture. What do these symbols tell us about Kateri Tekakwitha?

Kateri Tekakwitha

Kateri Tekakwitha was born in 1656 in Auriesville, New York. She lost her parents to an outbreak of smallpox when she was only four. She herself was left with scars and suffered the loss of some eyesight. When priests visited her village, Tekakwitha heard the call of Jesus. She was baptized at the age of 20, despite the opposition of her family and others in her Mohawk tribe of the Iroquois nation. Many could not understand her decision and her refusal to follow the ways of the Mohawks, and they insulted her and made life difficult for her. But she had the courage to continue to live her faith.

She left her home to live in a settlement of Catholic villages in Canada. There she took a vow to remain a virgin, and she dedicated herself entirely to God. She lived a life of prayer and fasting, and she cared for people who were poor and elderly. After her death in 1680, many who prayed to her reported miracles.

In 1980 Kateri Tekakwitha was the first Native American to be declared blessed—the step before sainthood. Her feast day is April 17.

Personal Decisions

On a separate sheet of paper, write about a time you made a difficult choice that people didn't understand or agree with. Why was it important to you?

Sacred Site

A shrine at Auriesville, in upstate New York, honors the place where the Jesuit priest Isaac Jogues and his companions, René Goupil and Jean de la Lande, were martyred, and where Kateri Tekakwitha lived. The Auriesville shrine has statues of Saint Isaac Jogues and Tekakwitha, memorials on the sites of the martyrdoms, Stations of the Cross, and a retreat house.

Name _____ Date _____

Art Print 24 depicts the reference to seven levels of Heaven, from those condemned to Hell to those chosen to be among God. What do you envision Heaven to be like?

Jesus Judges All

The Gospel of Matthew has a famous description of how Jesus will judge us at the end of time.

All the nations will be assembled before him [Jesus]. And he will separate them one from another, as a shepherd separates the sheep from the goats. He will place the sheep on his right and the goats on his left.

Then the king [Jesus] will say to those on his right, "Come, you who are blessed by my Father. Inherit the kingdom prepared for you from the foundation of the world. For I was hungry and you gave me food, I was thirsty and you gave me drink, a stranger and you welcomed me, naked and you clothed me, ill and you cared for me, in prison and you visited me." Then the righteous will answer him and say, "Lord, when did we see you hungry and feed you, or thirsty and give you drink? When did we see you a stranger and welcome you, or naked and clothe you? When did we see you ill or in prison, and visit you?" And the king will say to them in reply, "Amen I say to you, whatever you did for one of the least of my brothers, you did for me."

Then he will say to those on the left, "Depart from me . . . For I was hungry and you gave me no food, I was thirsty and you gave me no drink, a stranger and you gave me no welcome, naked and you gave me no clothing, ill and in prison, and you did not care for me. . . ." And these will go off to eternal punishment, but the righteous to eternal life.

adapted from Matthew 25:32–46

Acting in Faith

Reflect on a time you practiced one of the Corporal Works of Mercy.

_____

_____

_____

Name _____ Date _____

Art Print 25 shows Jesus' disciples receiving the Holy Spirit. They were filled with courage to go out into the world to speak God's Word. Has there been a time when you felt afraid to do something? How did you get over your fear?

Celebrating Pentecost

Before they received the power of the Holy Spirit, the disciples were probably discouraged. Jesus was no longer with them. How could they carry his message into the world without him?

After Jesus' Ascension, the disciples were gathered together. Suddenly the room was filled with a great rushing wind. Above the head of each person, a tongue of fire appeared. The disciples were filled with the desire and the strength to continue the mission begun by Jesus Christ.

At this time Jerusalem was filled with visitors from many different places, some as far away as Rome. The disciples left the room and addressed the crowd. Suddenly each visitor understood what was being said, as if the disciples had been speaking in that person's native language. *adapted from Acts of the Apostles 2:1–13*

In giving witness to Jesus, the disciples began to carry his mission to the world. The Holy Spirit brought the disciples the strength, confidence, and willingness to teach others about the promise of Salvation through Jesus Christ. We as Catholics are also called to carry on this mission. The Holy Spirit is active in our lives today also. He helps us bring people together and care for one another. On the lines below, list some examples of the ways the Holy Spirit is active in your life in the things you do to care for others.

_____

_____

_____

_____

_____

Glossary

A

Abba an informal name for *father* in Aramaic, the language Jesus spoke. It is like *dad* in English. When Jesus spoke to God the Father, he called him "Abba." [Abba]

absolution the forgiveness we receive from God through the priest in the Sacrament of Penance and Reconciliation [absolución]

Advent the four weeks before Christmas. It is a time of joyful preparation for the celebration of the Incarnation, Jesus' birth as our Savior, and a time for anticipating the coming of Jesus Christ at the end of time. [Adviento]

Advocate Jesus' name for the Holy Spirit. The Holy Spirit comforts us, speaks for us in difficult times, and makes Jesus present to us. [Abogado]

Alleluia a prayer of praise to God. It is usually sung as the Gospel Acclamation before the proclamation of the Gospel Reading at Mass except during Lent. [Aleluya]

All Saints Day November 1, the day on which the Church honors all who have died and now live with God as saints in Heaven. This group includes those who are officially recognized as saints as well as many unknown people who after a good life have died and now live in God's presence. The feast celebrates our union with those who have gone before us and points to our ultimate goal of union with God. [Día de Todos los Santos]

All Souls Day November 2, the day on which the Church prays that all friends of God who have died may rest in peace. Those who have died may need purification in Purgatory before living fully in God's presence. Our prayers and good works can help them in this process. Along with All Saints Day, this feast reminds us that all who love God, living and dead, are united in living communion with Jesus Christ and with one another. [Día de los Fieles Difuntos]

almsgiving the practice of giving money to those in need as an act of love [limosna, dar]

altar the table in the church on which the priest celebrates Mass, where the sacrifice of Christ on the cross is made present in the Sacrament of the Eucharist. The altar represents two aspects of the mystery of the Eucharist. It is the place where Jesus Christ offers himself for our sins and where he gives us himself as our food for eternal life. [altar]

ambo a raised stand from which a person reads the Word of God during Mass [ambón]

Amen the Hebrew word used to conclude Jewish and Christian prayers. It means "This is true," "So be it," or "Let it be so." We end prayers with *Amen* to show that we mean what we have just said. [Amén]

angel a spiritual creature who worships God in Heaven. Angels serve God as messengers. They tell us of God's plans for our Salvation. [ángel]

Angelus a Catholic devotion recited three times a day—morning, noon, and evening. The devotion reflects on the mystery of the Incarnation—the coming of the angel to Mary, her acceptance of the invitation to be the mother of Jesus, and the Word made flesh. [Ángelus]

Annunciation the announcement to Mary by the angel Gabriel that God had chosen her to be the mother of Jesus. When Mary agreed, the Son of God became man in her. The Feast of the Annunciation is celebrated on March 25, nine months before Christmas. [Anunciación]

Anointing of the Sick one of the seven sacraments. In this sacrament a sick person is anointed with holy oil and receives the strength, peace, and courage to overcome the difficulties associated with illness. Through this sacrament Jesus brings the sick person spiritual healing and forgiveness of sins. If it is God's will, healing of the body is given as well. [Unción de los enfermos]

apostle one of twelve chosen men who accompanied Jesus in his ministry and were witnesses to the Resurrection. *Apostle* means "one sent." These were the men sent to preach the Gospel to the whole world. [apóstol]

Apostles' Creed a statement of Christian belief that developed out of a creed used in Baptism in Rome. The Apostles' Creed lists simple statements of belief in God the Father, Jesus Christ the Son, and the Holy Spirit. It is the basis for the profession of faith used in Baptism today. [Credo de los Apóstoles]

apostolic one of the four Marks of the Church. The Church is apostolic because it continues to hand on the teaching of the apostles through their successors, the bishops, in union with the successor of Saint Peter, the pope. [apostólico]

Ark of the Covenant the sacred box God commanded Moses to build (Exodus 25:10–16), made of acacia wood to hold the restored tablets of the Law [Arca de la alianza]

Ascension the entry of Jesus into God's presence in Heaven. In the Acts of the Apostles, it is written that Jesus, after his Resurrection, spent 40 days on earth, instructing his followers. He then returned to his Father in Heaven. [Ascensión]

Ash Wednesday the first day of Lent, on which we receive ashes on our foreheads. The ashes remind us to prepare for Easter by repenting and showing sorrow for the choices we make that offend God and hurt our relationships with others. [Miércoles de Ceniza]

assembly the People of God when they are gathered together to worship him [asamblea]

Assumption Mary's being taken, body and soul, into Heaven. Mary had a special relationship with her Son, Jesus, from the very beginning, when she conceived him. Catholics believe that because of this relationship, she enjoys a special participation in Jesus' Resurrection and has been taken into Heaven where she now lives with him. We celebrate this event in the Feast of the Assumption on August 15. [Asunción]

B

Baptism the first of the seven sacraments. Baptism frees us from Original Sin and is necessary for Salvation. Baptism gives us new life in Jesus Christ through the Holy Spirit. The celebration of Baptism consists of immersing a person in water while declaring that the person is baptized in the name of the Father, the Son, and the Holy Spirit. [Bautismo]

baptismal font The water vessel where the Sacrament of Baptism is celebrated. The baptismal font may be located in a separate baptistery, near the entrance of the church, or in the midst of the community. [pila bautismal]

basic rights the human rights a government should protect, such as religious liberty, personal freedom, access to necessary information, right to life, and protection from terror and torture. [derechos humanos básicos]

basilica the term used to designate a certain church of historical significance in a local area. Major basilicas are in Rome and are designated churches of ancient origin that serve as places of pilgrimage. Minor basilicas are designated churches that have historical or devotional importance in local areas throughout the world. [basílica]

Beatitudes the teachings of Jesus in the Sermon on the Mount in Matthew's Gospel. The Beatitudes are eight ways of living the Christian life. They are the fulfillment of the commandments given to Moses. These teachings present the way to true happiness. [Bienaventuranzas]

Bible the collection of books containing the truths of God's revelation to us. These writings were inspired by the Holy Spirit and written by human beings. The Bible is made up of the 46 books in the Old Testament and 27 books in the New Testament. [Biblia]

bishop a man who has received the fullness of Holy Orders. As a successor to the original apostles, he takes care of the Church and is a principal teacher in it. [obispo]

Blessed Sacrament the Eucharist that has been consecrated by the priest at Mass. It is kept in the tabernacle to adore and to be taken to those who are sick. [Santísimo Sacramento]

blessing a prayer that calls for God's power and care upon some person, place, thing, or special activity [bendición]

Body and Blood of Christ the Bread and Wine that have been consecrated by the priest at Mass. In the Sacrament of the Eucharist, all of the risen Lord Jesus Christ—body, blood, soul, and divinity—is present in the form of Bread and Wine. [Cuerpo y Sangre de Cristo]

Bread of Life a title that Jesus gives himself in John 6:33–35. Jesus is the Bread of the Eucharist. He becomes spiritual food for the faithful. [pan de vida]

C

Canaan the name of the land between Syria and Egypt in which the Israelites settled [Caná]

canonize to declare that a Christian who has died is already a saint in Heaven and may be looked to as a model of Christian life who may intercede for us [canonizar]

capital sins those sins that can lead us to more serious sin. They are pride, covetousness, envy, anger, gluttony, lust, and sloth. [pecados capitales]

cast lots to throw down small stones or pebbles called lots to help determine a decision needing divine guidance. Lots were cast to choose the disciple to replace Judas in Acts of the Apostles 1:23–26. Roman soldiers also cast lots to divide Jesus' clothing among them as in John 19:24. [echar a suertes]

catechumen a person being formed in the Christian life through instruction and by the example of the parish community. Through conversion and maturity of faith, a catechumen is preparing to be welcomed into the Church at Easter through the Sacraments of Baptism, Confirmation, and the Eucharist. [catecúmeno]

catholic one of the four Marks of the Church. The Church is catholic because Jesus is fully present in it and because Jesus has given the Church to the whole world. It is universal. [católico]

celebrant a bishop or priest who leads the people in praying the Mass. A deacon who baptizes or witnesses a marriage is also a celebrant. [celebrante]

celebrate worshiping, praising, and thanking God for what he has done for us with prayers and songs, especially in the celebration of the Eucharist. [celebrar]

character a permanent spiritual mark. Character shows that a person has a new relationship with Jesus and a special standing in the Church. Baptism, Confirmation, and Holy Orders each have a specific permanent character and therefore may be received only once. [carácter]

charity a virtue given to us by God that helps us love God above all things and our neighbor as ourselves [caridad]

chastity the integration of our physical sexuality with our spiritual nature. Chastity helps us to be completely human, able to give to others our whole life and love. All people, married and single, are called to practice chastity. [castidad]

chasuble the visible liturgical vestment worn by the bishop or priest at Mass. The newly ordained priest receives a chasuble as part of the ordination ritual. [casulla]

Chosen People the people set apart by God to have a special relationship with him. God first formed a Chosen People when he made a covenant, or solemn agreement, with Abraham. He reaffirmed the Covenant through Moses at Mount Sinai. The covenant is fulfilled in Jesus and his Church. [pueblo elegido]

Chrism a perfumed oil, consecrated by a bishop, that is used in the Sacraments of Baptism, Confirmation, and Holy Orders. Anointing with Chrism signifies the call of the baptized to the threefold ministry of priest, prophet, and king. [crisma]

Christ a title that means "anointed with oil." It is from a Greek word that means the same thing as the Hebrew word *Messiah*, or "anointed." It is the name given to Jesus after the Resurrection when he completed his mission as priest, prophet, and king. [Cristo]

Christian the name given to all those who have been anointed through the gift of the Holy Spirit in Baptism and have become followers of Jesus Christ [cristiano]

Christmas the feast of the birth of Jesus (December 25) [Navidad]

Church the People of God throughout the whole world, or diocese (the local Church), or the Assembly of those called together to worship God. The Church is one, holy, catholic, and apostolic. [Iglesia]

clergy those men who are set apart as sacred ministers to serve the Church through Holy Orders [clero]

commandment a standard, or rule, for living as God wants us to live. Jesus summarized all the commandments into two: love God and love your neighbor. [mandamiento]

communal prayer the worship of God together with others. The Liturgy of the Hours and the Mass are the main forms of communal prayer. [oración común]

Communion of Saints the unity of all, dead or living, who have been saved in Jesus Christ. The Communion of Saints is based on our one faith, and it is nourished by our participation in the Eucharist. [Comunión de los Santos]

community Christians who are gathered in the name of Jesus Christ to receive his grace and live according to his values. [comunidad]

compassion God's fundamental attitude toward his people. This is best seen in Jesus' reaching out to heal those in need. Acting with compassion and mercy toward those in need identifies a person as belonging to God. [compasión]

confession the act of telling our sins to a priest in the Sacrament of Penance and Reconciliation. The sacrament itself is sometimes referred to as confession. [confesión]

Confirmation the sacrament that completes the grace we receive in Baptism. It seals, or confirms, this grace through the seven Gifts of the Holy Spirit that we receive as part of Confirmation. This sacrament also makes us better able to participate in the worship and apostolic life of the Church. [Confirmación]

conscience the inner voice that helps each of us to judge the morality of our own actions. It guides us to follow God's law by doing good and avoiding evil. [consciencia]

consecration the making of a thing or a person to be special to God through a prayer or blessing. At Mass the words of the priest are a consecration of the bread and wine that become the Body and Blood of Christ. People or objects set apart for God in a special way are also consecrated. For example, churches and altars are consecrated for use in liturgy,

and bishops are consecrated as they receive the fullness of the Sacrament of Holy Orders. [consagración]

contrition the sorrow we feel when we know that we have sinned, followed by the decision not to sin again. Perfect contrition arises from a love that loves God above all else. Imperfect contrition arises from other motives. Contrition is the most important act of the penitent preparing to celebrate the Sacrament of Penance and Reconciliation. [contrición]

conversion a radical or serious change of the whole life, away from sin and toward God. The call to change of heart is a key part of the preaching of Jesus. Throughout our entire lives, Jesus calls us to change in this way. [conversión]

Corporal Works of Mercy kind acts by which we help our neighbors with their everyday material needs. Corporal Works of Mercy include feeding the hungry, finding a home for the homeless, clothing the naked, visiting the sick and those in prison, giving alms to the poor, and burying the dead. [obras corporales de misericordia]

counsel one of the seven Gifts of the Holy Spirit. Counsel helps us to make correct choices in life through reflection, discernment, consultation, and advisement. [consejo]

covenant a solemn agreement between people or between people and God. God made covenants with humanity through agreements with Noah, Abraham, and Moses. These covenants offered Salvation. God's new and final covenant was established through Jesus' life, Death, Resurrection, and Ascension. *Testament* is another word for *covenant*. [alianza]

covet the excessive desire to possess something of value belonging to another person to the point of letting envy destroy the relationship [codiciar]

creation God's act of making everything that exists outside himself. Creation is everything that exists. God said that all of creation is good. [creación]

Creator God, who made everything that is and whom we can come to know through everything he created [Creador]

creed a brief summary of what people believe. The word *creed* comes from the Latin *credo*, "I believe." The Nicene Creed is the most important summary of Christian beliefs. [credo]

crosier the staff carried by a bishop that shows he cares for us in the same way that a shepherd cares for his sheep. It also reminds us that he represents Jesus, the Good Shepherd. [báculo]

crucified the way in which Jesus was put to death, nailed to a cross. As the crucified one, Jesus died for the sake of the world. [crucificado]

culture the collection of knowledge, belief, and behavior of a particular group of people. Culture expresses the shared attitudes, values, goals, and social practices of the group. To take root in a culture, the Gospel must be adapted to live in that culture as well as transform it. [cultura]

D

deacon a man ordained through the Sacrament of Holy Orders to the ministry of service in the Church. Deacons help the bishop and priests by serving in the various charitable practices of the Church. They help by proclaiming the Gospel and preaching and by assisting at the Liturgy of the Eucharist. Deacons also celebrate Baptism, bless marriages, and preside at funerals. [diácono]

detraction the act of talking about the faults and sins of another person to someone who has no reason to hear this and cannot help the person. Detraction damages the reputation of another person without any intent to help that person. [detracción]

diocese the members of the Church in a particular area, united in faith and the sacraments, and gathered under the leadership of a bishop [diócesis]

disciple a person who has accepted Jesus' message and tries to live as he did, sharing his mission, his suffering, and his joys [discípulo]

discipleship for Christians, the willingness to answer the call to follow Jesus. The call is received in Baptism, nourished in the Eucharist, and practiced in service to the world. [discipulado]

discrimination the act of mistreating other people because of how they look or act, or just because they are different [discriminación]

Dismissal the part of the Concluding Rites of the Mass in which the people are sent forth by the priest or deacon to do good works and praise and bless God [despedida]

Divine Praises a series of praises beginning with "Blessed be God," traditionally prayed at the end of the worship of the Blessed Sacrament in benediction [alabanzas de desagravio]

Divine Providence the guidance of God over all he has created. Divine Providence exercises care for all creation and guides it toward its final perfection. [Divina Providencia]

Doctor of the Church a man or a woman recognized as a model teacher of the Christian faith [Doctor de la Iglesia]

domestic church the Christian home, which is a community of grace and prayer and a school of human virtues and Christian charity [Iglesia doméstica]

Doxology from two Greek words *doxa*, "glory," and *logos*, "word" or "saying." In the liturgy it is our way of giving praise to God for being who he is and for what he has done and will do. [doxología]

E

Easter the celebration of the bodily raising of Jesus Christ from the dead. Easter is the festival of our redemption and the central Christian feast, the one from which other feasts arise. [Pascua]

Eastern Catholic Churches a group of churches that developed in the Near East (in countries such as Lebanon) that are in union with the Roman Catholic Church but have their own liturgical, theological, and administrative traditions. They show the truly catholic nature of the Church, which takes root in many cultures. [Iglesias Católicas Orientales]

Easter Vigil the celebration of the first and greatest Christian feast, the Resurrection of Jesus. It occurs on the first Saturday evening after the first full moon of spring. During this night watch before Easter morning, catechumens are baptized, confirmed, and receive Eucharist for the first time. [Vigilia Pascual]

Emmanuel a Hebrew name from the Old Testament that means "God with us." In Matthew's Gospel, Jesus is called *Emmanuel*. [Emanuel]

encyclical a letter written by the pope and sent to the whole Church and sometimes to the whole world. It expresses Church teaching on some specific and important issue. [encíclica]

envy a feeling of resentment or sadness because someone has a quality, a talent, or a possession that we want. Envy is one of the seven capital sins, and it is contrary to the Tenth Commandment. [envidia]

Epiphany the day on which we celebrate the visit of the Magi to Jesus after his birth. This is the day that Jesus was revealed as the Savior of the whole world. [Epifanía]

epistle a letter written by Saint Paul or another leader to a group of Christians in the early Church. Twenty-one of the 27 books of the New Testament are epistles. The Second Reading at Mass on Sundays and holy days is always from one of these books. [epistola]

eternal life living happily with God in Heaven when we die in grace and friendship with him. Jesus calls all people to eternal life. [vida eterna]

Eucharist the sacrament in which we give thanks to God for giving us the consecrated Bread and Wine that become the Body and Blood of Jesus Christ. This sacrament brings us into union with Jesus Christ and his saving Death and Resurrection. [Eucaristía]

Eucharistic liturgy the public worship, held by the Church, in which the consecrated Bread and Wine become the Body and Blood of Jesus Christ. The Sunday celebration of the Eucharistic liturgy is at the heart of Church life. [liturgia eucarística]

Eucharistic Prayer during the Mass the liturgical expression of praise and thanksgiving for all that God has done in creation and in the Paschal Mystery (Christ's dying and rising from the dead for all) and through the Holy Spirit [Plegaria Eucarística]

euthanasia an action taken or omitted that purposely results in the death of a sick, disabled, or dying person. It is always gravely wrong and morally unacceptable. [eutanasia]

Evangelists the four men credited with writing the Gospels of Matthew, Mark, Luke, and John [evangelista]

evangelization the proclamation, or declaring by word and by example, of the good news about the Salvation we have received in Jesus Christ. Evangelization is a sharing of our faith with others, both those who do not know Jesus and those who are called to follow Jesus more closely. [evangelización]

examination of conscience the act of prayerfully thinking about what we have said or done in light of what the Gospel asks of us. We also think about how our actions may have hurt our relationship with God or with others. An examination of conscience is an important part of our preparing to celebrate the Sacrament of Penance and Reconciliation. [examen de conciencia]

Exile the period in the history of Israel between the destruction of Jerusalem in 587 B.C. and the return to Jerusalem in 537 B.C. During this time many of the Jewish people were forced to live in Babylon, far from home. [exilio]

Exodus God's liberation of the Hebrew people from slavery in Egypt and his leading them to the Promised Land [Éxodo]

F

faith a gift of God that helps us to believe in him. We profess our faith in the creed, celebrate it in the sacraments, live by it through our good conduct of loving God and our neighbor, and express it in prayer. [fe]

fasting limiting the amount we eat for a period of time to express sorrow for sin and to make ourselves more aware of God's action in our lives. Adults 18 years old and older fast on Ash Wednesday and Good Friday. The practice is also encouraged as a private devotion at other times of penitence. [ayuno]

fear of the Lord one of the seven Gifts of the Holy Spirit. This gift leads us to a sense of wonder and awe in the presence of God because we recognize his greatness. [temor de Dios]

Feast of the Holy Family celebrated on the Sunday that falls within the octave of Christmas, or, if no Sunday falls within the octave, on December 30. The feast celebrates the family of Jesus, Mary, and Joseph as a model for all Catholic families. [Fiesta de la Sagrada Familia]

forgiveness the willingness to be kind to those who have hurt us but have then shown that they are sorry. In the Lord's Prayer, we pray that since God will forgive us for our sins, we are able to forgive those who have hurt us. [perdón]

fortitude the strength to choose to do the right thing even when that is difficult. Fortitude is one of the four central human virtues, called the cardinal virtues, by which we guide our conduct through faith and the use of reason. It is also one of the Gifts of the Holy Spirit. [fortaleza]

free will the ability to choose to do good because God has made us like him. Our free will is what makes us truly human. Our exercise of free will to do good increases our freedom. Using free will to choose sin makes us slaves to sin. [libre albedrío]

Fruits of the Holy Spirit the demonstration through our actions that God is alive in us. Saint Paul lists the Fruits of the Holy Spirit in Galatians 5:22–23: love, joy, peace, patience, kindness, generosity, faithfulness, gentleness, and self-control. Church Tradition has added goodness, modesty, and chastity to make a total of 12. [frutos del Espíritu Santo]

G

Garden of Eden a garden created by God, filled with trees and lush vegetation, where God first placed Adam and Eve and from which they were later expelled [Jardín del Edén]

genuflect to show respect in church by touching a knee to the ground, especially before the Blessed Sacrament in the tabernacle [genuflexión, hacer la]

gestures the movements we make, such as the Sign of the Cross or bowing, to show our reverence during prayer [gestos]

gift of peace the peace that Jesus gives to us that flows from his relationship with his Father. This is the peace that the world cannot give, for it is the gift of Salvation that only Jesus can give. [don de la paz]

Gifts of the Holy Spirit the permanent willingness, given to us by the Holy Spirit, that makes it possible for us to do what God asks of us. The Gifts of the Holy Spirit are drawn from Isaiah 11:1–3. They include wisdom, understanding, counsel, fortitude, knowledge, and fear of the Lord. Church Tradition has added piety to make a total of seven. [dones del Espíritu Santo]

God the Father, Son, and Holy Spirit, one God in three distinct Persons. God created all that exists. He is the source of Salvation, and he is truth and love. [Dios]

godparent a witness to Baptism who assumes the responsibility for helping the baptized person along the road of Christian life [padrino/madrina de Bautismo]

Gospel the good news of God's mercy and love that we experience by hearing the story of Jesus' life, Death, and Resurrection. The story is passed on in the teaching ministry of the Church as the source of all truth and right living. It is presented to us in four books in the New Testament: the Gospels of Matthew, Mark, Luke, and John. [Evangelio]

grace the gift from God given to us without our meriting it. Sanctifying grace fills us with God's life and makes it possible for us always to be his friends. Grace is the Holy Spirit alive in us, helping us to live our Christian vocation. Grace helps us to live as God wants us to live. [gracia]

Great Commandment Jesus' commandment that we are to love both God and our neighbor as we love ourselves. Jesus tells us that this commandment sums up everything taught in the Old Testament. [Mandamiento Mayor, el]

guardian angel the angel who has been appointed to protect, pray for, and help a person live a holy life [ángel de la guarda]

H

habit the distinctive clothing worn by members of religious orders. It is a sign of the religious life and a witness to poverty. [hábito]

Heaven union with God the Father, Son, and Holy Spirit in life and love that never ends. Heaven is a state of complete happiness and the goal of the deepest wishes of the human heart. [cielo]

Hebrews the descendants of Abraham, Isaac, and Jacob, who were enslaved in Egypt. God helped Moses lead the Hebrews out of slavery. (*See* Israelites.) [hebreos]

Hell a life of total separation from God forever. In his infinite love for us, God can only desire our Salvation. Hell is the result of the free choice of a person to reject God's love and forgiveness once and for all. [infierno]

holiness the fullness of Christian life and love. All people are called to holiness, which is made possible by cooperating with God's grace to do his will. As we do God's will, we are transformed more and more into the image of the Son, Jesus Christ. [santidad]

holy one of the four Marks of the Church. It is the kind of life we live when we share in the life of God, who is all holiness. The Church is holy because it is united with Jesus Christ. [santa]

Holy Communion the consecrated Bread and Wine that we receive at Mass, which is the Body and Blood of Jesus Christ. It brings us into union with Jesus and his saving Death and Resurrection. [Sagrada Comunión]

Holy Days of Obligation the principal feast days, other than Sundays, of the Church. On Holy Days of Obligation, we celebrate the great things that God has done for us through Jesus and the saints. Catholics are obliged to participate in the Eucharist on these days, just as we are on Sundays. [días de precepto]

Holy Family the family of Jesus as he grew up in Nazareth. It included Jesus; his mother, Mary; and his foster father, Joseph. [Sagrada Familia]

Holy of Holies the holiest part of the Temple in Jerusalem. The high priest entered this part of the Temple once a year to address God and ask his forgiveness for the sins of the people. [Sanctasanctórum]

Holy Orders the sacrament through which the mission given by Jesus to his apostles continues in the Church. The sacrament has three degrees: deacon, priest, and bishop. Through the laying on of hands in the Sacrament of Holy Orders, men receive a permanent sacramental mark that calls them to minister to the Church. [sacramento del Orden]

Holy Spirit the third Person of the Trinity, who is sent to us as our helper and, through Baptism and Confirmation, fills us with God's life. Together with the Father and the Son, the Holy Spirit brings the divine plan of Salvation to completion. [Espíritu Santo]

Holy Thursday the Thursday of Holy Week on which the Mass of the Lord's Supper is celebrated, commemorating the institution of the Eucharist. The season of Lent ends with the celebration of this Mass. [Jueves Santo]

holy water water that has been blessed and is used as a sacramental to remind us of our Baptism [agua bendita]

Holy Week the celebration of the events surrounding Jesus' establishment of the Eucharist, his suffering, Death, and Resurrection. Holy Week commemorates Jesus' triumphal entry into Jerusalem on Palm Sunday, the gift of himself in the Eucharist on Holy Thursday, his Death on Good Friday, and his Resurrection at the Easter Vigil on Holy Saturday. [Semana Santa]

Homily the explanation by a bishop, a priest, or a deacon of the Word of God in the liturgy. The Homily relates the Word of God to our life as Christians today. [homilía]

honor giving God or a person the respect that they are owed. God is given this respect as our Creator and Redeemer. All people are worthy of respect as children of God. [honrar]

hope the confidence that God will always be with us, make us happy now and forever, and help us to live so that we will be with him forever [esperanza]

human condition the general state of humankind. While the human family is created in the image and likeness of God, it is also wounded by sin and often rejects the grace won by Jesus Christ. So while called by God to the highest good, too often human behavior leads to personal and social destruction. [condición humana]

I

idolatry in the Bible, the pagan worship of physical images given adoration as gods. For Christians today idolatry occurs whenever someone honors and reveres something in place of God. This can mean giving honor to power, pleasure, race, ancestors, or money over that which is owed to God. [idolatría]

Incarnation the Son of God, Jesus, being born as a full human being in order to save us. The Son of God, the second Person of the Trinity, is both true God and true man. [Encarnación]

indulgence a lessening of the punishment due for sins that have been forgiven. Indulgences move us toward our final purification, when we will live with God forever. [indulgencia]

inspired influenced by the Holy Spirit. The human authors of Scripture were influenced by the Holy Spirit. The creative inspiration of the Holy Spirit made sure that the Scripture was written according to the truth God wants us to know for our Salvation. [inspirado]

interpretation an explanation of the words of Scripture, combining human knowledge and the teaching office of the Church under the guidance of the Holy Spirit [interpretación]

Islam the third great religion, along with Judaism and Christianity, professing belief in one God. *Islam* means "submission" to that one God. [islamismo]

Israelites the descendants of Abraham, Isaac, and Jacob. God changed Jacob's name to "Israel," and Jacob's twelve sons and their children became the leaders of the twelve tribes of Israel. (*See* Hebrews.) [israelitas]

J

Jerusalem city conquered by David in 1000 B.C. to serve as his capital. David also made it the center of worship by bringing in the Ark of the Covenant, which held the tablets of the Law. [Jerusalén]

Jesse Tree an Advent activity that helps us to prepare to celebrate Jesus' birth. A small real or artificial tree is decorated with images of Jesus' ancestors beginning with Jesse of Bethlehem, father of King David. The image is based on Isaiah 11:1 *But a shoot shall sprout from the stump of Jesse, and from his roots a bud shall blossom.* [tronco de Jesé]

Jesus the Son of God, who was born of the Virgin Mary and who died and was raised from the dead for our Salvation. He returned to God and will come again to judge the living and the dead. *Jesus* means "God saves." [Jesús]

Jews the name given to the Hebrew people, from the time of the exile to the present. The name means "the people who live in the territory of Judah," the area of Palestine surrounding Jerusalem. [judíos]

Joseph the foster father of Jesus, who was engaged to Mary when the angel announced that Mary would have a child through the power of the Holy Spirit. In the Old Testament, Joseph was the son of Jacob, who was sold into slavery in Egypt by his brothers and then saved them from starvation when famine came. [José]

Judaism the name of the religion of Jesus and all of the people of Israel after they returned from exile in Babylon and built the second Temple [judaísmo]

justice the virtue that guides us to give to God and others what is due them. Justice is one of the four central human virtues, called the cardinal virtues, by which we guide our Christian life. [justicia]

K

Kingdom of God God's rule over us, announced in the Gospel and present in the Eucharist. The beginning of the Kingdom here on earth is mysteriously present in the Church, and it will come in completeness at the end of time. [reino de Dios]

Kingdom of Heaven the Gospel of Matthew's term for the Kingdom of God. The Kingdom of God is God's rule over us, announced in the Gospel and present in the Eucharist. [reino de los cielos]

knowledge one of the seven Gifts of the Holy Spirit. This gift helps us to know what God asks of us and how we should respond. [conocimiento]

L

laity those who have been made members of Christ in Baptism and who participate in the priestly, prophetic, and kingly functions of Christ in his mission to the whole world. The laity is distinct from the clergy, whose members are set apart as ministers to serve the Church. [laicado]

Lamb of God the title for Jesus that emphasizes his willingness to give up his life for the Salvation of the world. Jesus is the Lamb without blemish or sin who delivers us through his sacrificial Death. [cordero de Dios]

Last Supper the last meal Jesus ate with his disciples on the night before he died. At the Last Supper, Jesus took Bread and Wine, blessed them, and said that they were his Body and Blood. Jesus' Death and Resurrection, which we celebrate in the Eucharist, was anticipated in this meal. [Última Cena]

Lectionary for Mass the official book that contains all the Scripture readings used in the Liturgy of the Word [Leccionario]

Lent the 40 days before Easter (not counting Sundays) during which we prepare, through prayer, fasting, and giving aid to those who are poor, to change our lives and live the Gospel more completely [Cuaresma]

Light of the World a name that helps us see that Jesus is the light that leads us to the Father. Jesus lights up our minds and hearts, replacing sin and darkness with the knowledge of God. [luz del mundo]

liturgical year the celebration throughout the year of the mysteries of the Lord's birth, life, Death, Resurrection, and Ascension. The cycle of the liturgical year constitutes the basic rhythm of the Christian's life of prayer. [año litúrgico]

liturgy the public prayer of the Church that celebrates the wonderful things God has done for us in Jesus Christ, our high priest, and the way in which he continues the work of our Salvation. The original meaning of *liturgy* was "a public work or service done for the people." [liturgia]

Liturgy of the Eucharist the part of the Mass in which the bread and wine are consecrated and become the Body and Blood of Jesus Christ. We then receive Christ in Holy Communion. [Liturgia de la Eucaristía]

Liturgy of the Hours the public prayer of the Church to praise God and sanctify the day. It includes an office of readings before sunrise, morning prayer at dawn, evening prayer at sunset, and prayer before going to bed. The chanting of psalms makes up a major portion of each of these services. [Liturgia de las Horas]

Liturgy of the Word the part of the Mass in which we listen to God's Word from the Bible and consider what it means for us today. The Liturgy of the Word can also be a public prayer and proclamation of God's Word that is not followed by the Liturgy of the Eucharist. [Liturgia de la Palabra]

M

Magisterium the living, teaching office of the Church. This office, through the bishops and with the pope, provides an authentic interpretation of the Word of God. It ensures faithfulness to the teaching of the apostles in matters of faith and morals. [Magisterio]

Magnificat Mary's song of praise to God for the great things he has done for her and for his plans for us through Jesus [Magníficat]

manna the food provided by God when the Israelites were in the desert [maná]

Marks of the Church the four most important aspects of the Church found in the Nicene Creed. According to the Nicene Creed, the Church is one, holy, catholic, and apostolic. [atributos de la Iglesia]

Mary the mother of Jesus. She is called blessed and "full of grace" because God chose her to be the mother of the Son of God, the second Person of the Trinity. [María]

Mass the most important sacramental celebration of the Church, established by Jesus at the Last Supper as a remembrance of his Death and Resurrection. At Mass we listen to God's Word from the Bible and receive Jesus Christ in the consecrated Bread and Wine that are his Body and Blood. [misa]

Matrimony a solemn agreement between a woman and a man to be partners for life, both for their own good and for raising children. Marriage is a sacrament when the agreement is properly made between baptized Christians. [Matrimonio]

memorial a remembrance of events that have taken place in the past. We recall these events because they continue to affect us because they are part of God's saving plan for us. Every time we remember these events, we make God's saving action present. [conmemoración]

mercy the gift to be able to respond to those in need with care and compassion. The gift of mercy is a grace given to us by Jesus Christ. [misericordia]

Messiah a title that means "anointed with oil." It is from a Hebrew word that means the same thing as the Greek word *Christ*. "Messiah" is the title that was given to Jesus after the Resurrection, when he had completed his mission as priest, prophet, and king. [Mesías]

ministry service or work done for others. Ministry is done by bishops, priests, and deacons, who are all ordained to ministry in the celebration of the sacraments. All those baptized are called to a variety of ministries in the liturgy and in service to the needs of others. [ministerio]

miracle the healing of a person, or an occasion when nature is controlled that can only be recognized as God's action in the world. Jesus' miracles are signs of the presence of God's kingdom. [milagro]

mission the work of Jesus Christ that is continued in the Church through the Holy Spirit. The mission of the Church is to proclaim Salvation in Jesus' life, Death, Resurrection, and Ascension. [misión]

monastery a place where men or women live out their solemn vows of poverty, chastity, and obedience in a stable community life. They spend their days in public prayer, work, and meditation. [monasterio]

moral choice a choice to do what is right or not do what is wrong. We make moral choices because they help us grow closer to God and because we have the freedom to choose what is right and avoid what is wrong. [opción moral]

moral law a rule for living that has been established by God and people in authority who are concerned about the good of all. Moral laws are based on God's direction to us to do what is right and avoid what is wrong. Some moral laws are "written" in the human heart and can be known through our own reasoning. Other moral laws have been revealed to us by God in the Old Testament and in the new Law given by Jesus. [ley moral]

mortal sin a decision to turn away from God by doing something that we know is seriously wrong. For a sin to be mortal, it must be a very serious offense, the person must know how serious the sin is, and the person must freely choose to do it anyway. [pecado mortal]

Muslim a follower of the religion of Islam. *Muslim* means "one who submits to God." [musulmán]

mystery a religious truth that we can know only through God's revelation and that we cannot fully understand. Our faith is a mystery that we profess in the Creed and celebrate in the liturgy and sacraments. [misterio]

Mystical Body of Christ the members of the Church formed into a spiritual body and bound together by the life communicated by Jesus Christ through the sacraments. Christ is the center of this body and the source of life. In it we are all united. Each member of the body receives from Christ gifts fitting for him or her. [Cuerpo Místico de Cristo]

N

Nativity scene a picture or crèche that shows Jesus, Mary, and Joseph in the stable after the birth of Jesus as described in the Gospels of Matthew and Luke [escena de la Natividad del Señor]

natural law the moral law that is "written" in the human heart. We can know natural law through our own reason because the Creator has placed the knowledge of it in our hearts. It can provide the solid foundation on which we can make rules to guide our choices in life. Natural law forms the basis of our fundamental rights and duties and is the foundation for the work of the Holy Spirit in guiding our moral choices. [ley natural]

neighbor according to Jesus, everyone, as each person is made in God's image. We are all meant to develop mutually supportive relationships. [prójimo]

New Testament the 27 books of the second part of the Bible which tell of the teaching, ministry, and saving events of the life of Jesus. The four Gospels present Jesus' life, Death, and Resurrection. The Acts of the Apostles tells the story of Jesus' Ascension into Heaven. It also shows how Jesus' message of Salvation spread through the growth of the Church. Various letters instruct us in how to live as followers of Jesus Christ. The Book of Revelation offers encouragement to Christians living through persecution. [Nuevo Testamento]

Nicene Creed the summary of Christian beliefs developed by the bishops at the first two councils of the Church, held in A.D. 325 and 381. It is the Creed shared by most Christians in the East and in the West. [Credo Niceno]

O

obedience the act of willingly following what God asks us to do for our Salvation. The Fourth Commandment requires children to obey their parents, and all people are required to obey civil authority when it acts for the good of all. To imitate the obedience of Jesus, members of religious communities make a special vow of obedience. [obediencia]

obey to follow the teachings or directions given by God or by someone who has authority over us [obedecer]

oil of catechumens the oil blessed by the bishop during Holy Week and used to anoint catechumens. This anointing strengthens them on their path to initiation into the Church. Infants are anointed with this oil right before they are baptized. [óleo de los catecúmenos]

oil of the sick the oil blessed by the bishop during Holy Week and used in the Sacrament of the Anointing of the Sick, which brings spiritual and, if it is God's will, physical healing [óleo de los enfermos]

Old Testament the first 46 books of the Bible, which tell of God's Covenant with the people of Israel and his plan for the Salvation of all people. The first five books are known as the Torah. The Old Testament is fulfilled in the New Testament, but God's Covenant presented in the Old Testament has permanent value and has never been revoked. [Antiguo Testamento]

one one of the four Marks of the Church. The Church is one because of its source in the one God and because of its founder, Jesus Christ. Jesus, through his Death on the cross, united all to God in one body. Within the unity of the Church, there is great diversity because of the variety of the gifts given to its members. [una]

ordained men who have received the Sacrament of Holy Orders so that they may preside at the celebration of the Eucharist and serve as leaders and teachers of the Church [ordenado]

Ordinary Time the longest liturgical season of the Church. It is divided into two periods—the first after the Christmas season and the second after Pentecost. The first period focuses on Jesus' childhood and public ministry. The second period focuses on Christ's reign as King of Kings. [Tiempo Ordinario]

ordination the rite of the Sacrament of Holy Orders, by which a bishop gives to men, through the laying on of hands, the ability to minister to the Church as bishops, priests, and deacons [ordenación]

Original Sin the consequence of the disobedience of the first human beings. They disobeyed God and chose to follow their own will rather than God's will. As a result human beings lost the original blessing God had intended and became subject to sin and death. In Baptism we are restored to life with God through Jesus Christ although we still experience the effects of Original Sin. [pecado original]

P

Palm Sunday the celebration of Jesus' triumphant entry into Jerusalem on the Sunday before Easter. It begins a week-long commemoration of the saving events of Holy Week. [Domingo de Ramos]

parable one of the simple stories that Jesus told to show us what the Kingdom of God is like. Parables present images drawn from everyday life. These images show us the radical choice we make when we respond to the invitation to enter the Kingdom of God. [parábola]

parish a stable community of believers in Jesus Christ who meet regularly in a specific area to worship God under the leadership of a pastor [parroquia]

Paschal Mystery the work of Salvation accomplished by Jesus Christ through his Passion, Death, and Resurrection. The Paschal Mystery is celebrated in the liturgy of the Church, and its saving effects are experienced by us in the sacraments. [Misterio Pascual]

Passion the suffering and Death of Jesus. [pasión]

Passover the Jewish festival that commemorates the delivery of the Hebrew people from slavery in Egypt. In the Eucharist, we celebrate our passover from death to life through Jesus' Death and Resurrection. [Pascua Judía]

pastor a priest who is responsible for the spiritual care of the members of a parish community. It is the job of the pastor to see that the Word of God is preached, the faith is taught, and sacraments are celebrated. [pastor]

patriarchs the leaders of families and clans within ancient Israel. More specifically, in biblical studies, patriarchs are the founders of the Hebrew people described in Genesis chapters 12 through 50. Prominent among the patriarchs are Abraham, Isaac, Jacob, and Jacob's 12 sons. [patriarcas]

peacemaker a person who teaches us to be respectful in our words and actions toward one another [paz, los que trabajar por la]

penance the turning away from sin with a desire to change our life and more closely live the way God wants us to live. We express our penance externally by praying, fasting, and helping those who are poor. This is also the name of the action that the priest asks us to take or the prayers that he asks us to pray after he absolves us in the Sacrament of Penance and Reconciliation. (*See* Sacrament of Penance and Reconciliation.) [penitencia]

Penitential Act a formula of general confession asking for God's mercy said at Mass. The priest may lead the assembly in praying the *Confiteor* ("I confess to almighty God...") or a threefold invocation echoed by "Lord have mercy . . . Christ have mercy . . . Lord have mercy" in English or in Greek. [acto penitencial]

Pentecost the 50th day after Jesus was raised from the dead. On this day the Holy Spirit was sent from Heaven, and the Church was born. It is also the Jewish feast that celebrated the giving of the Ten Commandments on Mount Sinai 50 days after the Exodus. [Pentecostés]

People of God another name for the Church. In the same way that the people of Israel were God's people through the Covenant he made with them, the Church is a priestly, prophetic, and royal people through the new and eternal covenant with Jesus Christ. [pueblo de Dios]

personal prayer the kind of prayer that rises up in us in everyday life. We pray with others in the liturgy, but in addition we can listen and respond to God through personal prayer every moment of our lives. [oración personal]

personal sin a sin we choose to commit, whether serious (mortal) or less serious (venial). Although the consequences of Original Sin leave us with a tendency to sin, God's grace, especially through the sacraments, helps us to choose good over sin. [pecado personal]

petition a request to God, asking him to fulfill a need. When we share in God's saving love, we understand that every need is one that we can ask God to help us with through petition. [petición]

Pharaoh the Egyptian word for "Great House," referring to the royal palace of the king of Egypt. Then references to *Pharaoh* became known for the king himself, just as "White House" might refer to the president. Pharaoh was both the political and religious leader of Egypt. [faraón]

piety one of the seven Gifts of the Holy Spirit. This gift calls us to be faithful in our relationships both with God and with others. Piety helps us to love God and to behave responsibly and with generosity and affection toward others. [piedad]

plague a natural calamity or disease that is seen as being inflicted by God as a remedial event to make people more conscious of their duties toward God and one another. (Numbers 14:37) In Exodus 7:14—12:30, the plagues inflicted on the Egyptians are seen as the means by which God convinced the Egyptians to free the Hebrew people from slavery [plaga]

pope the bishop of Rome, successor of Saint Peter, and leader of the Roman Catholic Church. Because he has the authority to act in the name of Christ, the pope is called the Vicar of Christ. The pope and all of the bishops together make up the living, teaching office of the Church, the Magisterium. [Papa]

praise the expression of our response to God, not only for what he does, but simply because he is. In the Eucharist the whole Church joins with Jesus Christ in expressing praise and thanksgiving to the Father. [alabanza]

prayer the raising of our hearts and minds to God. We are able to speak to and listen to God in prayer because he teaches us how to pray. [oración]

Precepts of the Church those positive requirements that the pastoral authority of the Church has determined are necessary to provide a minimum effort in prayer and the moral life. The Precepts of the Church ensure that all Catholics move beyond the minimum by growing in love of God and love of neighbor. [preceptos de la Iglesia]

presbyter a word that originally meant "an elder or a trusted advisor to the bishop." From this word comes the English word *priest*, one of the three degrees of the Sacrament of Holy Orders. All the priests of a diocese under the bishop form the presbyterate. [presbítero]

pride a false image of ourselves that goes beyond what we deserve as God's creation. Pride puts us in competition with God. It is one of the seven capital sins. [soberbia]

priest a man who has accepted God's special call to serve the Church by guiding it and building it up through the ministry of the Word and the celebration of the sacraments [sacerdote]

priesthood all the people of God who have been given a share of the one mission of Christ through the Sacraments of Baptism and Confirmation. The ministerial priesthood, which is made up of those men who have been ordained bishops and priests in Holy Orders, is essentially different from the priesthood of all the faithful because its work is to build up and guide the Church in the name of Christ. [sacerdocio]

Promised Land the land first promised by God to Abraham. It was to this land that God told Moses to lead the Chosen People after they were freed from slavery in Egypt and received the Ten Commandments at Mount Sinai. [Tierra prometida]

prophet one called to speak for God and call the people to be faithful to the Covenant. A major section of the Old Testament presents, in 18 books, the messages and actions of the prophets. [profeta]

prudence the virtue that directs us toward the good and helps us to choose the correct means to achieve that good. When we act with prudence, we carefully and thoughtfully consider our actions. Prudence is one of the cardinal virtues that guide our conscience and influence us to live according to the Law of Christ. [prudencia]

psalm a prayer in the form of a poem, written to be sung in public worship. Each psalm expresses an aspect of the depth of human prayer. Over several centuries 150 psalms were assembled into the Book of Psalms in the Old Testament. Psalms were used in worship in the Temple in Jerusalem, and they have been used in the public worship of the Church since its beginning. [salmo]

Purgatory a state of final cleansing after death of all of our human imperfections to prepare us to enter into the joy of God's presence in Heaven [purgatorio]

R

racism the opinion that race determines human traits and capacities and that a particular race has an inherent, or inborn, superiority. Discrimination based on a person's race is a violation of human dignity and a sin against justice. [racismo]

Real Presence the way in which the risen Jesus Christ is present in the Eucharist under the form of Bread and Wine. Jesus Christ's presence is called real because in the Eucharist his Body and Blood, soul and divinity, are wholly and entirely present. [Presencia Real]

reconciliation the renewal of friendship after that friendship has been broken by some action or lack of action. In the Sacrament of Penance and Reconciliation, through God's mercy and forgiveness, we are reconciled with God, the Church, and others. [reconciliación]

Redeemer Jesus Christ, whose life, sacrificial Death on the cross, and Resurrection from the dead set us free from the slavery of sin and bring us redemption [Redentor]

redemption our being set free from the slavery of sin through the life, sacrificial Death on the cross, and Resurrection from the dead of Jesus Christ [redención]

reform to put an end to a wrong by introducing a better or changed course of action. The prophets called people to reform their lives by returning to being faithful to their Covenant with God. [reformarse]

religious life a state of life recognized by the Church. In the religious life, men and women freely respond to a call to follow Jesus by living the vows of poverty, chastity, and obedience in community with others. [vida religiosa]

repentance our turning away from sin with a desire to change our lives and live more closely as God wants us to live. We express our penance externally by prayer, fasting, and helping those who are poor. [arrepentimiento]

Resurrection the bodily raising of Jesus Christ from the dead on the third day after his Death on the cross. The Resurrection is the crowning truth of our faith. [Resurrección]

Revelation God's communication of himself to us through the words and deeds he has used throughout history to show us the mystery of his plan for our Salvation. This revelation reaches its completion in his sending of his Son, Jesus Christ. [revelación]

rite one of the many forms followed in celebrating liturgy in the Church. A rite may differ according to the culture or country where it is celebrated. *Rite* also means "the special form for celebrating each sacrament." [rito]

Rosary a prayer in honor of the Blessed Virgin Mary. When we pray the Rosary, we meditate on the mysteries of Jesus Christ's life while praying the Hail Mary on five sets of ten beads and the Lord's Prayer on the beads in between. In the Latin Church, praying the Rosary became a way for ordinary people to reflect on the mysteries of Christ's life. [Rosario]

S

Sabbath the seventh day, when God rested after finishing the work of Creation. The Third Commandment requires us to keep the Sabbath holy. For Christians the Sabbath became Sunday because it was the day Jesus rose from the dead and the new creation in Jesus Christ began. [Sabat]

sacrament one of seven ways through which God's life enters our lives through the work of the Holy Spirit. Jesus gave us three sacraments that bring us into the Church: Baptism, Confirmation, and the Eucharist. He gave us two sacraments that bring us healing: Penance and Reconciliation and Anointing of the Sick. He also gave us two sacraments that help members serve the community: Matrimony and Holy Orders. [sacramento]

sacramental an object, a prayer, or a blessing given by the Church to help us grow in our spiritual life [sacramental]

Sacrament of Penance and Reconciliation the sacrament in which we celebrate God's forgiveness of sin and our reconciliation with God and the Church. Penance includes sorrow for the sins we have committed, confession of sins, absolution by the priest, and doing the penance that shows our willingness to amend our ways. [sacramento de la Penitencia y de la Reconciliación]

Sacraments at the Service of Communion the Sacraments of Holy Orders and Matrimony. These two sacraments contribute to the personal Salvation of individuals by giving them a way to serve others. [sacramentos al servicio de la comunidad]

Sacraments of Healing the Sacraments of Penance and Reconciliation and Anointing of the Sick, by which the Church continues the healing ministry of Jesus for soul and body [sacramentos de curación]

Sacraments of Initiation the sacraments that are the foundation of our Christian life. We are born anew in Baptism, strengthened by Confirmation, and receive in the Eucharist the food of eternal life. By means of these sacraments, we receive an increasing measure of divine life and advance toward the perfection of charity. [sacramentos de iniciación]

sacrifice a ritual offering of animals or produce made to God by the priest in the Temple in Jerusalem. Sacrifice was a sign of the people's adoration of God, giving thanks to God, or asking for his forgiveness. Sacrifice also showed union with God. The great high priest, Christ, accomplished our redemption through the perfect sacrifice of his Death on the cross. [sacrificio]

Sacrifice of the Mass the sacrifice of Jesus on the cross, which is remembered and mysteriously made present in the Eucharist. It is offered in reparation for the sins of the living and the dead and to obtain spiritual or temporal blessings from God. [Sacrificio de la misa]

saint a holy person who has died united with God. The Church has said that this person is now with God forever in Heaven. [santo]

Salvation the gift, which God alone can give, of forgiveness of sin and the restoration of friendship with him [salvación]

sanctifying grace the gift of God, given to us without our earning it, that unites us with the life of the Trinity and heals our human nature, wounded by sin. Sanctifying grace continues the work of making us holy that began at our Baptism. [gracia santificante]

Savior Jesus, the Son of God, who became man to forgive our sins and restore our friendship with God. *Jesus* means "God saves." [Salvador]

scriptorium the room in a monastery in which books were copied by hand. Often, beautiful art was created on the page to illustrate the story. [scriptorium]

Scriptures the holy writings of Jews and Christians collected in the Old and New Testaments of the Bible [Sagrada Escritura]

seal of confession also called the "sacramental seal." It declares that the priest is absolutely forbidden to reveal under any circumstances any sin confessed to him in the Sacrament of Penance and Reconciliation. [sigilo sacramental]

seraphim the Heavenly beings who worship before the throne of God. One of them purified the lips of Isaiah with a burning coal so that he could speak for God (Isaiah 6:6–7). [serafines]

Sermon on the Mount the words of Jesus, written in chapters 5 through 7 of the Gospel of Matthew, in which Jesus reveals how he has fulfilled God's Law given to Moses. The Sermon on the Mount begins with the eight Beatitudes and includes the Lord's Prayer. [Sermón de la montaña]

sexism a prejudice or discrimination based on sex, especially discrimination against women. Sexism leads to behaviors and attitudes that foster a view of social roles based only on sex. [sexismo]

Sign of Peace the part of the Mass in which we offer a gesture of peace to one another as we prepare to receive Holy Communion. This signifies our willingness to be united in peace before we receive our Lord. [rito de la paz]

Sign of the Cross the gesture that we make that signifies our belief in God the Father, the Son, and the Holy Spirit. It is a sign of blessing, a confession of faith, and identifies us as followers of Jesus Christ. [señal de la cruz]

sin a deliberate thought, word, deed, or failure to act that offends God and hurts our relationships with other people. Some sin is mortal and needs to be confessed in the Sacrament of Penance and Reconciliation. Other sin is venial, or less serious. [pecado]

slander a false statement that harms the reputation of someone and makes other people think badly of that person. Slander is an offense against the Eighth Commandment. [calumnia]

sloth a carelessness of heart that leads a person to ignore his or her development as a person, especially spiritual development and a relationship with God. Sloth is one of the seven capital sins, and it is contrary to the First Commandment. [pereza]

solidarity the principle that all people exist in equal dignity as children of God. Therefore, individuals are called to commit themselves to working for the common good in sharing material and spiritual goods. [solidaridad]

Son of God the title revealed by Jesus that indicates his unique relationship to God the Father. The revelation of Jesus' divine sonship is the main dramatic development of the story of Jesus of Nazareth as it unfolds in the Gospels. [Hijo de Dios]

soul the part of us that makes us human and an image of God. Body and soul together form one unique human nature. The soul is responsible for our consciousness and for our freedom. The soul does not die and is reunited with the body in the final resurrection. [alma]

Spiritual Works of Mercy the kind acts through which we help our neighbors meet needs that are more than material. The Spiritual Works of Mercy include instructing, advising, consoling, comforting, forgiving, and bearing wrongs with patience. [obras espirituales de misericordia]

Stations of the Cross a tool for meditating on the final hours of Jesus' life, from his condemnation by Pilate to his Death and burial. We do this by moving to representations of 14 incidents, each one based on the traditional sites in Jerusalem where these incidents took place. [Estaciones del Vía Crucis]

stewardship the careful and responsible management of something entrusted to one's care, especially the goods of creation, which are intended for the whole human race. The sixth Precept of the Church makes clear our part in this stewardship by requiring us to provide for the material needs of the Church, according to our abilities. [administración]

T

tabernacle the container in which the Blessed Sacrament is kept so that Holy Communion can be taken to those who are sick and dying. *Tabernacle* is also the name of the tent sanctuary in which the Israelites kept the Ark of the Covenant from the time of the Exodus to the construction of Solomon's Temple. [sagrario]

temperance the cardinal virtue that helps us to control our attraction to pleasure so that our natural desires are kept within proper limits. This moral virtue helps us choose to use created goods in moderation. [templanza]

Temple the house of worship of God, first built by Solomon. The Temple provided a place for the priests to offer sacrifice, to adore and give thanks to God, and to ask for forgiveness. It was destroyed and rebuilt. The second Temple was also destroyed and was never rebuilt. Part of the outer wall of the Temple mount remains to this day in Jerusalem. [Templo, judío]

temptation an attraction, from outside us or inside us, that can lead us to disobey God's commands. Everyone is tempted, but the Holy Spirit helps us to resist temptation and choose to do good. [tentación]

Ten Commandments the ten rules given by God to Moses on Mount Sinai that sum up God's Law and show us what is required to love God and our neighbor. By following the Ten Commandments, the Hebrews accepted their Covenant with God. [Diez Mandamientos]

Theological Virtues those virtues given us by God and not by human effort. They are faith, hope, and charity. [virtudes teologales]

Torah the Hebrew word for "instruction" or "law." It is also the name of the first five books of the Old Testament: Genesis, Exodus, Leviticus, Numbers, and Deuteronomy. [Torá]

transubstantiation when the bread and wine become the Body and Blood of Jesus Christ. When the priest speaks the words of consecration, the substance of the bread and wine is changed into the substance of Christ's Body and Blood. [transubstanciación]

trespasses unlawful acts committed against the property or rights of another person or acts that physically harm a person [ofensas]

Trinity the mystery of the existence of God in three Persons: the Father, the Son, and the Holy Spirit. Each Person is God, whole and entire. Each is distinct only in the relationship of each to the others. [Trinidad]

U

understanding one of the seven Gifts of the Holy Spirit. This gift helps us make the right choices in life and in our relationships with God and with others. [entendimiento]

universal Church the entire Church as it exists throughout the world. The people of every diocese, along with their bishops and the pope, make up the universal Church. [Iglesia universal]

V

venial sin a choice we make that weakens our relationships with God or with others. Venial sin wounds and lessens the divine life in us. If we make no effort to do better, venial sin can lead to more serious sin. Through our participation in the Eucharist, venial sin is forgiven, strengthening our relationships with God and with others. [pecado venial]

viaticum the Eucharist that a dying person receives. It is spiritual food for the last journey we make as Christians, the journey through death to eternal life. [viático]

Vicar of Christ the title given to the pope who, as the successor of Saint Peter, has the authority to act in Christ's place. A vicar is someone who stands in for and acts for another. [Vicario de Cristo]

virtue an attitude or a way of acting that enables us to do good [virtud]

Visitation Mary's visit to Elizabeth to share the good news that Mary is to be the mother of Jesus. Elizabeth's greeting of Mary forms part of the Hail Mary. During this visit Mary sings the Magnificat, her praise of God. [Visitación]

vocation the call each of us has in life to be the person God wants us to be and the way we each serve the Church and the Kingdom of God. Each of us can live out his or her vocation as a layperson, as a member of a religious community, or as a member of the clergy. [vocación]

vow a deliberate and free promise made to God by people who want especially to dedicate their lives to God. Their vows give witness now to the kingdom that is to come. [voto]

Vulgate the Latin translation of the Bible by Saint Jerome from the Hebrew and Greek in which it was originally written. Most Christians of Saint Jerome's day no longer spoke Hebrew or Greek. The common language, or vulgate, was Latin. [Vulgata]

W

wisdom one of the seven Gifts of the Holy Spirit. Wisdom helps us to understand the purpose and plan of God and to live in a way that helps to bring about this plan. It begins in wonder and awe at God's greatness. [sabiduría]

Wisdom Literature the Old Testament books of Job, Proverbs, Ecclesiastes, the Song of Songs, Wisdom, and Sirach. The purpose of these books is to give instruction on ways to live and how to understand and cope with the problems of life. [Libros Sapienciales]

witness the passing on to others, by our words and by our actions, the faith that we have been given. Every Christian has the duty to give witness to the good news about Jesus Christ that he or she has come to know. [testimonio]

worship the adoration and honor given to God in public prayer [culto]

Y

Yahweh the name of God in Hebrew, which God told Moses from the burning bush. *Yahweh* means "I am who am" or "I cause to be all that is." [Yavé]

Index

A
Abba, 251
Abraham, 16, 209, 233, 267
absolution, 107, 201, 251
Act of Contrition, 108, 189
Act of Faith, 192
Act of Hope, 192
Act of Love, 192
Adam, 10, 11, 16, 34
adoration, prayer of, 186
Advent, 57–60, 152, 153–56, 234, 251
Advocate, 52, 251.
    See also Holy Spirit
Agony in the Garden, 197
All Saints Day, 27, 152, 177–80, 251
All Souls Day, 27, 152, 177–80, 251
Alleluia, 251
almsgiving, 117, 251
Alphonsus Liguori, Saint, 31, 32
altar, 101, 251
ambo, 251
Amen, 251
angel, 158, 162, 251
    guardian, 260
Angelus, 251
Annunciation, 196, 251
Anointing of the Sick, Sacrament of the, 28, 41, 106, 112, 113, 201, 252
apostle, 27, 52, 64, 233, 236, 242, 243, 252.
    See also specific apostles
Apostles' Creed, 36, 37, 64, 66, 190, 252
apostolic, 252
Ark of the Covenant, 237, 252, 272
Ascension, 27, 83, 147, 149 197, 233, 236, 249, 252
Ash Wednesday, 27, 117, 161, 252
assembly, 95, 252
Assumption, 83, 197, 252
Augustine, Saint, 1, 2

B
Babylon, 154, 258
Baptism, Sacrament of, 28, 40, 45–50, 52, 55, 59, 200, 232, 252
    Baptism of Jesus, 196
baptismal font, 59, 252
Barabbas, 244
basic rights, 253
basilica, 73, 253
Beatitudes, 23, 25, 209, 253
Beltrame Quattrocchi, Luigi and Maria Corsini, Blessed, 76
Benedict XVI, Pope, 65
Bernadette, Saint, 91, 92, 112
Bible, 4, 15, 184–85, 253. *See also* Ten Commandments
    human condition, 10
    parts of, 184–85, 227
    passage location, 185, 227
    Vulgate, 274
bishop, 2, 53, 64, 71, 201, 236, 253
Blessed Sacrament, 253
blessing, 204, 253
    prayer of, 186
body, 138
    respecting, 137
Body and Blood of Christ, 59, 95, 101, 241, 253, 255. *See also* Eucharist, Sacrament of the
bread and wine, 255
bread of life, 240, 253.
    See also Jesus

C
Canaan, 253
candles, 46, 48
canonize, 253
capital sins, 253, 268, 272.
    See also sin
cardinal virtues, 212
Carr, George, 238
Carrying of the Cross, 197
cast lots, 253

catechumen, 253
catholic, 254
celebrant, 254
celebrate, 254
character, 71, 254
charity, 212, 254
chastity, 137, 212, 254
chasuble, 254
child of light, 48
children, 22
choices. *See also* good choices; moral choice
Chosen People, 254
Chrism, 40, 71, 254
Chrism Mass, 113
Christ, 112, 254.
    See also Jesus
Christian, 17, 254
    mission as, 52
Christianity, 16, 17
Christmas, 27, 87–90, 152, 157–60, 239, 254.
    See also Advent
    Mass, 89
Church, the, 254
    Christ's mission, 34
    diversity in, 235
    Eastern tradition, 67
    leaders, 73
    nature of, 63–68
    pope's role within, 65
    Precepts of, 205
    roles in, 64, 230
    stewards, 47
    unity in, 235
clergy, 64, 254
Collect, 202
commandment, 254. *See also* Ten Commandments
    Great Commandment, 208, 260
    new commandment, 209
communal, 186, 254
Communion. *See also* Holy Communion; Service of Communion, Sacraments at the
    Rite, 101, 204

Acknowledgments

Excerpts from the *New American Bible with Revised New Testament and Psalms.* Copyright © 1991, 1986, 1970 Confraternity of Christian Doctrine, Inc., Washington, DC. Used with permission. All rights reserved. No part of the *New American Bible* may be reprinted without permission in writing from the copyright holder.

The English translation of the Act of Contrition from *Rite of Penance* © 1974, International Commission on English in the Liturgy Corporation (ICEL); the English translation of the *Salve, Regina* from *A Book of Prayers* © 1982, ICEL; the English translation of Prayer Before Meals and Prayer After Meals from *Book of Blessings* © 1988; the English translation of the Nicene Creed and Apostles' Creed from *The Roman Missal* © 2010, ICEL. All rights reserved.

For more information related to the English translation of the *Roman Missal, Third Edition,* see www.loyolapress.com/romanmissal.

Loyola Press has made every effort to locate the copyright holders for the cited works used in this publication and to make full acknowledgment for their use. In the case of any omissions, the publisher will be pleased to make suitable acknowledgments in future editions.

Art and Photography

When there is more than one picture on a page, positions are abbreviated as follows: (t) top, (c) center, (b) bottom, (l) left, (r) right, (bg) background, (bd) border.

Photos and illustrations not acknowledged are either owned by Loyola Press or from royalty-free sources including but not limited to Alamy, Corbis/Veer, Getty Images, Jupiterimages, PunchStock, Thinkstock, and Wikipedia Commons. Loyola Press has made every effort to locate the copyright holders for the cited works used in this publication and to make full acknowledgment for their use. In the case of any omissions, the publisher will be pleased to make suitable acknowledgments in future editions.

Frontmatter: i Rafael Lopez. **ii** Anni Betts. **iii**(tr) Zvonimir Atletic/Shutterstock. **iii**(bl) Tom Merton/Alamy. **iii**(br) Anni Betts. **iv**(tl) Warling Studios. **iv**(tr) ©iStockphoto.com/kulicki. **iv**(cr) iStockphoto/Thinkstock. **iv**(bl) ©iStockphoto.com/ FeliciaMontoya. **iv**(br) Christina Balit.

©iStockphoto.com: 2(b) sunnyfrog. **4**(c) mipan. **6** Jamesbowyer. **7**(c) mxtama. **10**(t) jane. **11**(b) FotografiaBasica. **17**(t) ghstuder. **22** JBryson. **25**(t) Vaida_P. **25**(b) SaulHerrera. **35**(b) bo1982. **36** gbh007. **37** kwerensia. **40**(b) princessdlaf. **43**(t) Elenathewise. **43**(b) gfxwork. **46**(t) sebastianiov. **56**(t) sebastianiov. **57**(t) Hogie. **59** anthony_taylor. **78** lisafx. **80**(t) Broncox. **80**(b) barsik. **87**(t) MissHibiscus. **87**(b) Maljuk. **94**(t) dra_schwartz. **94**(b) nicoolay. **95**(b) princessdlaf. **119**(b) art-4-art. **125**(t) MsSponge. **125**(b) JMSetzler. **131**(t) gbh007. **133**(t) philhxc. **137** pixdeluxe. **144** Yuri_Arcurs. **152**(b) Luso. **153**(b) stoupa. **157**(r) Vgm6. **161**(b) dlerick. **168** stevenallan. **171**(c) Pyast. **172** innlens. **175** AlbertSmirnov. **177**(b) FeliciaMontoya. **179**(b) BCFC. **181**(t) kulicki. **181**(ct) ggodby. **181**(cb) Liliboas. **181**(bl) gbh007. **182**(bl) princessdlaf. **182**(br) kryczka. **185** mahnken. **186–187**(cb) Liliboas. **186–187**(b) gbh007. **190–191**(bg) ggodby. **192–193**(bg) AVTG. **194**(bl) nicolecioe. **202**(br) dra_schwartz. **203**(t) dra_schwartz. **204**(t) kryczka. **210**(bl) tilo. **212–213**(bg) gavni. **214**(t) princessdlaf. **214**(b) GlobalP. **215**(br) MarkCoffeyPhoto. **216**(bl) jstudio. **219**(bg) catrinka81. **220–221**(bg) catrinka81. **224**(bg) catrinka81. **225** skeeg. **229** Cloudniners. **235** Illustrious.

Thinkstock: 1(t) iStockphoto. **3** iStockphoto. **12**(b) Creatas Images/ Creatas. **14**(t) Hemera. **15** George Doyle/Valueline. **17**(b) iStockphoto. **20**(t) Hemera Technologies/PhotoObjects.net. **20**(b) iStockphoto. **21** Jupiterimages/Brand X Pictures. **26**(b) Comstock Images/Comstock. **31**(t) iStockphoto. **49**(b) Hemera. **57**(b) iStockphoto. **75** David Sacks/Lifesize. **76**(b) Hemera. **81** Milk & Honey Creative/Brand X Pictures. **82** Jupiterimages/Creatas. **83**(bd) iStockphoto. **84** Hemera. **85**(t) iStockphoto. **88**(b) Hemera. **89** Hemera. **90**(b) Hemera. **93** Jupiterimages/Brand X Pictures. **96** Hemera. **98**(b) Hemera. **102** Jupiterimages/Polka Dot. **103**(b) iStockphoto. **104**(b) Hemera. **109**(b) iStockphoto. **110**(t) iStockphoto. **115**(bl) iStockphoto. **117**(b) iStockphoto. **120**(t) Hemera. **124–125**(b) iStockphoto. **126** Hemera. **127**(t) iStockphoto. **127**(b) Hemera. **128**(b) Jupiterimages/ Brand X Pictures. **130**(t) Digital Vision. **131**(bg) iStockphoto. **132** Hemera Technologies/AbleStock.com. **133**(bl) Hemera. **136**(t) Hemera. **136**(c) Jupiterimages/Photos.com. **138** iStockphoto. **140**(b) Jupiterimages/Comstock. **145**(t) iStockphoto. **145**(b) iStockphoto. **146**(t) Hemera Technologies/PhotoObjects.net. **146**(b) Jupiterimages/ Comstock. **149**(t) Hemera. **150**(t) iStockphoto. **153**(t) iStockphoto. **154**(bd) iStockphoto. **157**(b) Hemera. **158**(t) iStockphoto. **158–159**(b) Hemera/Thinkstock. **159**(t) Hemera Technologies/ PhotoObjects.net/Thinkstock. **162**(b) Thomas Northcut/Photodisc. **165**(bl) iStockphoto. **166–167** iStockphoto. **169**(br) Hemera. **173**(bl) Hemera. **181**(br) iStockphoto. **184**(t) iStockphoto. **184**(b) Hemera Technologies/PhotoObjects.net. **186**(t) iStockphoto. **186**(ct) iStockphoto/Thinkstock. **188–189**(bg) Hemera. **189**(t) Jupiterimages/Brand X Pictures. **197**(b) iStockphoto. **210–211**(b) Hemera. **211**(c) Thomas Northcut/Photodisc. **216–217, 221–222**(notes) iStockphoto. **217**(b) Jupiterimages/BananaStock.

Unit 1: 1(b) Bettmann/Corbis. **2**(t) Bettmann/Corbis. **4**(b) Tom Merton/Alamy. **5**(t) New Mexico State University Art Gallery Collection. Acc. #1969.3.6. **5**(b) Jupiterimages. **7**(t) Siede Preis/ Photodisc. **7**(bl) C Squared Studios/Photodisc. **7**(br) C Squared Studios/Photodisc. **8**(b) Blend Images/Alamy. **9** Corbis Photography/ Veer. **10**(b) Amanda Hall. **11**(t) Roman Accessories, from "Trachten der Voelker," 1864 (color litho), Kretschmer, Albert (1825–91)/Private Collection/The Bridgeman Art Library International. **12**(t) Photodisc. **13** Amos Morgan/Photodisc. **14**(b) Michael Newman/PhotoEdit. **16** Musee du Louvre, Paris/Art Resource, NY. **18**(t) Siede Preis/ Photodisc. **18**(b) Inmagine/Alamy. **19**(t) David Sanger Photography/ Alamy. **19**(b) AgnusImages.com. **23**(t) Wang, Elizabeth (Contemporary Artist)/Private Collection/© Radiant Light/The Bridgeman Art Library International. **23**(b) Phil Martin Photography. **24** Richard Koek/Stone/ Getty Images. **26**(t) Brother Michael Moran, C.P./Angel Studio. **27** SW Productions/Photodisc. **29**(t) James, Laura (Contemporary Artist)/ Private Collection/The Bridgeman Art Library International. **29**(b) Phil Martin Photography. **30**(b) Phil Martin Photography.

Unit 2: 31(b) Painting of St. Alphonsus Liguori and St. Gerard Majellan by J.W. Printon CSSR, courtesy of St. Alphonsus, Chicago, Illinois. **32**(t) Painting of St. Alphonsus Liguori and St. Gerard Majellan by J.W. Printon CSSR, courtesy of St. Alphonsus, Chicago, Illinois. **32**(b) Courtesy of Liguori Publications. **33** Ocean Photography/ Veer. **34** Apic/Hulton Archive/Getty Images. **35**(c) Erich Lessing/ Magnum Photos. **38**(t) StockphotoPro. **39** Datacraft-Sozaijiten/Alamy. **40**(t) Phil Martin Photography. **40**(c) Alan Oddie/PhotoEdit. **41** Top to bottom, (a) Royalty-free image. **41**(b) Alan Oddie/PhotoEdit. **41**(c) The Crosiers/Gene Plaisted, OSC. **41**(d) Ocean Photography/Veer. **41**(e) Anni Betts. **42** Mark Pearson/Alamy. **44**(t) The Crosiers/Gene Plaisted, OSC. **44**(b) Big Cheese Photo LLC/Alamy. **45** MarioPonta/ Alamy. **46–47**(b) Jupiterimages. **47**(t) Regina Kubelka. **48** Fuse/ PunchStock. **49**(t) Julie Lonneman. **50**(t) Christina Balit. **50**(b) Phil Martin Photography. **51** Stockbyte/Getty Images. **52** C Squared Studios/ Photodisc. **53**(t) Phil Martin Photography. **53**(b) www.colonialarts.com. **54** Bertrand Demee/Photographer's Choice/Getty Images. **56**(b) Phil Martin Photography. **57**(c) Jupiterimages. **58** WoodyStock/Alamy. **60**(t) Phil Martin Photography. **60**(b) W. P. Wittman Limited.

Unit 3: 61(b) Robert Harding Picture Library Ltd./Alamy. **62**(t) Robert Harding Picture Library Ltd./Alamy. **63** Borderlands/Alamy. **65**(t) Candace Beckwith/BigstockPhoto.com. **65**(bl) Zvonimir Atletic/ Shutterstock. **65**(b) Clipart.com. **66** W. P. Wittman Limited. **67** Courtesy of Dr. Elizabeth Lee Hudgins/iconsofthefaith.com. **68**(t) David Lees/Corbis. **68**(b) Femia Streefkerk/Flickr. **69** Jerry Lampen/Reuters/Corbis. **70**(t) Pavel Chichikov/Ponkawonka.

70 (b) Clipart.com. 71 The Crosiers/Gene Plaisted, OSC. 72 Todd Muskopf/Alamy. 74 (t) Cameramann International/Milton and Joan Mann. 74 (b) Phil Martin Photography. 76 (t) Private Collection. 76 (c) Private Collection. 77 (t) Carlos Davila/Alamy. 79 Michael D. O'Brien, www.studiobrien.com. 83 (t) Zvonimir Atletic/Shutterstock.com. 85 (b) Alexander Moreno Delgado/Flickr. 86 (b) Fancy/Alamy. 88 (t) Jupiterimages. 90 (t) Siede Preis/Photodisc.

Unit 4: 91 (b) Wikipedia. 92 (t) Archives Charmet/The Bridgeman Art Library International. 92 (c) Hemis/Alamy. 92 (b) Mary Evans Picture Library/Alamy. 95 (t) Warling Studios. 97 (t) Julie Hagan/Shutterstock.com. 97 (b) Christina Balit. 99 fStop/Alamy. 100 (t) Scala/Art Resource, NY. 101 Myrleen Ferguson Cate/PhotoEdit. 103 (t) Radiant Light/The Bridgeman Art Library International. 104 (t) The Crosiers/Gene Plaisted, OSC. 105 Saskia Massink/Bigstock.com. 106 Jim West/Alamy. 107 (t) Warling Studios. 108 Fancy/Alamy. 109 (t) The Crosiers/Gene Plaisted, OSC. 110 (b) Phil Martin Photography. 111 OJO Images Ltd./Alamy. 112 (t) Mary Evans Picture Library/Alamy. 112 (b) The Art Gallery Collection/Alamy. 113 (t) Judy Swazey, St. Martin of Tours Parish, San Jose, CA. 113 (b) Greg Kuepfer. 114 Blend Images/Alamy. 115 (t) Warling Studios. 115 (c) W. P. Wittman Limited. 115 (b) Clipart.com. 116 (t) Zvonimir Atletic/Shutterstock.com. 116 (b) Warling Studios. 117 (t) Siede Preis/Photodisc. 117 (c) Attila Kisbenedek/AFP/Getty Images. 118 The Art Gallery Collection/Alamy. 119 (t) Clipart.com. 120 (b) W. P. Wittman Limited.

Unit 5: 121 (b) Jim Lewis, www.icarusfurniture.com. 122 (t) Jim Lewis, www.icarusfurniture.com. 122 (b) The Crosiers/Gene Plaisted, OSC. 123 Blend Images/Alamy. 125 (c) Image Source/Alamy. 128 (t) Elizabeth Wang, T-00464A-CW-V4, "In the Mass Jesus greets with great affection all those who love and welcome Him," copyright © Radiant Light 2011, www.radiantlight.org.uk. 129 Image Source/Alamy. 130 (b) Phil Martin Photography. 134 (t) Private Collection/The Bridgeman Art Library International. 134 (b) Blend Images/Alamy. 135 ONOKY-Photononstop/Alamy. 136 (b) Image Source/Getty Images. 139 The Crosiers/Gene Plaisted, OSC. 140 (t) www.e-scoutcraft.com. 141 Ali Arman/Alamy. 142 (t) Amos Nattini/Private Collection/The Bridgeman Art Library International. 142 (b) The Crosiers/Gene Plaisted, OSC. 143 (b) Associated Press/Pier Paolo Cito. 147 (t) The Crosiers/Gene Plaisted, OSC. 147 (c) Steve Cole/Photodisc. 147 (b) Steve Cole/Photodisc. 148–149 C Squared Studios/Photodisc. 150 (b) Peter Casolino/Alamy.

Seasonal Sessions: 151 Julie Lonneman. 152 (t) Zvonimir Atletic/Shutterstock.com. 154 (t) Giraudon/The Bridgeman Art Library International. 155 (br) Cultura Photography/Veer. 156 blickwinkel/Alamy. 158 (c) Siede Preis/Photodisc. 160 W. P. Wittman Limited. 161 (t) The Crosiers/Gene Plaisted, OSC. 161 (c) Phil Martin Photography. 162 (t) © Guildhall Art Gallery, City of London/The Bridgeman Art Library International. 163 (t) Warling Studios. 163 (ct) Warling Studios. 163 (cb) Stockbyte/Getty. 163 (b) Siede Preis/Photodisc. 164 Warling Studios. 165 (t) Associated Press/Jeffrey Phelps. 165 (br) Mode Images Limited/Alamy. 167 (t) Clipart.com. 167 (c) ReligiousStock/Alamy. 169 (t) The Crosiers/Gene Plaisted, OSC. 169 (bl) Eder/Shutterstock.com. 170 (t) Thom Sund. 170–171 (b) OPIS/Shutterstock.com. 171 (t) Warling Studios. 173 (t) The Crosiers/Gene Plaisted, OSC. 173 (br) ColonialArts.com 174 (t) The Crosiers/Gene Plaisted, OSC. 174 (b) Courtesy of Br. Claude Lane, OSB of Mount Angel Abbey, Saint Benedict, Oregon. 176 The Crosiers/Gene Plaisted, OSC. 177 (t) Bobby Deal/RealDealPhoto/Shutterstock.com. 178 (t, b) C Squared Studios/Photodisc. 178 (c) Michael D. O'Brien, www.studiobrien.com. 179 (t) S. Meltzer/PhotoLink/Stockbyte. 180 National Gallery, London, UK/The Bridgeman Art Library International.

Endmatter: 182 (t) Siede Preis/Photodisc. 183 (l) Steve Heap/Shutterstock.com. 183 (r) Jupiterimages. 183 (b) Image Source/Alamy. 188 (br) Marc Hill/Alamy. 189 (b) Siede Preis/Photodisc. 190 (b) Jozef Sedmak/Shutterstock.com. 191 (t) Jupiterimages. 192 (t) Jupiterimages. 192 (b) Shutterstock.com. 193 (t) Image courtesy of Artazia.com. 194 (t) Loop Delay/Westend61/Corbis. 194 (br) Warling Studios. 195 Greg Kuepfer. 196 (ct) W. P. Wittman Ltd. 196 (cb) The Crosiers/Gene Plaisted, OSC. 196 (b) W. P. Wittman Ltd. 197 (t) Clipart.com. 198–199 (tl) Zvonimir Atletic/Shutterstock.com. 200 (tr) W. P. Wittman Ltd. 200 (cr) W. P. Wittman Ltd. 200 (br) Con Tanasiuk/Design Pics Inc./Alamy. 200–201 (b) Corey Hochachka/Alloy Photography/Veer. 201 Top to bottom (a) W. P. Wittman Ltd. 201 (b) W. P. Wittman Ltd.

201 (c) The Crosiers/Gene Plaisted, OSC. 201 (d) W. P. Wittman Ltd. 202 (t) Colorblind/Photodisc/Getty Images. 203 (b) Zvonimir Atletic/Shutterstock.com. 205 W. P. Wittman Ltd. 206 Vadim Kozlovsky/Shutterstock.com. 207 Warling Studios. 208 (t) michaeljung/Veer. 208–209 (b) Jupiterimages. 209 (br) IZA Stock/PunchStock. 210 (t) Erich Lessing/Art Resource, NY. 213 (br) Warling Studios. 215 (cl) C Squared Studios/Photodisc. 215 (cr) C Squared Studios/Photodisc. 215 (bl) Image Source/Alamy. 217 (t) Chubykin Arkady/Shutterstock.com. 218–219 (b) italianestro/Shutterstock.com. 219 (t) Image Source/Alamy. 220 (t) Desislava Dimitrova/Veer. 221 (br) Caroline Schiff/Blend Images/Getty Images. 222–223 (b) RTIMAGES/Veer. 223 (t) Jupiterimages. 224 (br) Image Source/Alamy. 226 © The Crosiers/Gene Plaisted, OSC. 228 © The Crosiers/Gene Plaisted, OSC. 230 Kantner's Illustrated Book of Objects. 231 Bandelin-Dacey Studios. 232 © The Crosiers/Gene Plaisted, OSC. 234 Yoshi Miyake. 236 © The Crosiers/Gene Plaisted, OSC. 237 Yoshi Miyake. 238 Courtesy Basilica of The National Shrine of the Immaculate Conception, Washington, DC. 239 © The Crosiers/Gene Plaisted, OSC. 240 © The Crosiers/Gene Plaisted, OSC. 241 © The Crosiers/Gene Plaisted, OSC. 242 © The Crosiers/Gene Plaisted, OSC. 243 Bandelin-Dacey Studios. 244 © The Crosiers/Gene Plaisted, OSC. 245 Yoshi Miyake. 246 Bandelin-Dacey Studios. 247 © The Crosiers/Gene Plaisted, OSC. 248 © The Crosiers/Gene Plaisted, OSC. 249 © The Crosiers/Gene Plaisted, OSC.

Name _____ Date _____

Art Print 17 shows Jesus and his disciples sharing in the Last Supper.
Why is sharing a meal important to you and your family?

The Eucharist Calls Us to Share

An ordained priest leads the celebration of the Eucharist. Jesus Christ is present through the priest. The Eucharistic liturgy remembers the sacrifice Jesus made for us. We participate by receiving the Eucharist, a **memorial,** or remembrance, of this sacrifice, which redeems our sins and offers us everlasting life.

According to Saint Paul, Christians cannot truly celebrate the Eucharist unless they are ready to love and share with one another. Paul was especially critical of those who were rich, who would gather with the community to eat but not to share what they had.

> Therefore, whoever eats the bread or drinks the cup of the Lord unworthily will have to answer for the body and blood of the Lord. A person should examine himself, and so eat the bread and drink the cup. For anyone who eats and drinks without discerning the body, eats and drinks judgment on him. *adapted from 1 Corinthians 11:27–29*

By "discerning the body," Paul means that those celebrating the Eucharist must understand that Jesus died for many people. To receive the Body and the Blood of Christ "worthily," we should be ready to live like Jesus.

Worthy of the Eucharist

On a separate sheet of paper, write ways in which you can act worthy of receiving the Eucharist.

Reading God's Word

Therefore, if you bring your gift to the altar, and there recall that your brother has anything against you, leave your gift there at the altar, go first and be reconciled with your brother, and then come and offer your gift.

Matthew 5:23–24

Name _____ Date _____

Art Print 18 shows Jesus revealing himself to his apostles after he is risen. Think of a time when you were at your lowest and you asked Jesus for help. How did you feel?

Jesus Brings Us Peace and Forgiveness

The apostles were gathered together after Jesus died, afraid of what the authorities might do to them as Jesus' followers.

On the evening of the first day of the week, when the doors were locked where the disciples were, Jesus appeared and said to them, "Peace be with you." He showed them his hands and his side. The disciples rejoiced when they saw the Lord. Jesus said to them again, "Peace be with you. As the Father has sent me, so I send you." Then, he breathed on them and said to them, "Receive the Holy Spirit. Whose sins you forgive are forgiven them, and whose sins you retain, are retained."

adapted from John 20:19–23

The risen Jesus brings peace. This gift of the Holy Spirit helps people live in harmony with others and with themselves. This is reconciliation, the returning of harmony to our broken relationships with God, with others, and even with ourselves. In the Gospel story, Jesus gives the apostles the authority to forgive sins and reconcile people with God and with one another. The Church celebrates that gift in the Sacrament of Reconciliation.

Learning to Forgive

Think about a time when you asked for forgiveness from someone whom you wronged. Then recall a time when someone asked for your forgiveness. Write a brief prayer to God, thanking him for the strength to forgive and to be forgiven yourself.

_____

_____

_____

_____

_____

_____

Name _____ Date _____

Art Print 19 shows Peter and John healing a man who was crippled, who becomes overjoyed with God's work. When was a time you thanked God for something great in your life?

The Apostles Heal in Jesus' Name

Now Peter and John were going up to the temple area for the three o'clock hour of prayer. And a man crippled from birth was carried and placed at the gate of the temple called "the Beautiful Gate" every day to beg for alms from the people who entered the temple. When he saw Peter and John about to go into the temple, he asked for alms. But Peter looked intently at him, as did John, and said, "Look at us." He paid attention to them, expecting to receive something from them. Peter said, "I have neither silver nor gold, but what I do have I give you: in the name of Jesus Christ the Nazorean, [rise and] walk." Then Peter took him by the right hand and raised him up, and immediately his feet and ankles grew strong. He leaped up, stood, and walked around, and went into the temple with them, walking and jumping and praising God. When all the people saw him walking and praising God, they recognized him as the one who used to sit begging at the Beautiful Gate of the temple, and they were filled with amazement and astonishment of what had happened to him.

Acts of the Apostles 3:1–10

The healed man's response to God's act was overwhelming joy, expressed in an outpouring of praise to God. God continues to heal in the Church through the Holy Spirit. By uniting our prayers with Jesus in the Spirit, God will always hear us and answer in some way.

Gratitude List

On a separate sheet of paper, list five things in your life that make you happy. Write a brief prayer to God, giving thanks for all he has done for you.

Link to Liturgy

Before we receive Holy Communion, we acknowledge our dependence on God. We pray, "Lord, I am not worthy that you should enter under my roof, but only say the word and my soul shall be healed."

© LOYOLAPRESS.

Name _____   Date _____

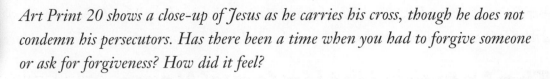

Art Print 20 shows a close-up of Jesus as he carries his cross, though he does not condemn his persecutors. Has there been a time when you had to forgive someone or ask for forgiveness? How did it feel?

Jesus Forgives

The week Jesus died began with his triumphal entry into Jerusalem on Palm Sunday as the people cried out, "Blessed is the king who comes in the name of the Lord." Later in the week Jesus shared a final meal with his disciples on Holy Thursday. That evening he was arrested. The next morning, Good Friday, Jesus came before Pilate.

When Jesus stood before Pilate to be judged, the crowd turned against Jesus and shouted for his crucifixion. Pilate told the crowd that Jesus had done nothing wrong. The crowd demanded the release of Barabbas, a criminal and murderer. Pilate did as the crowd asked. He released Barabbas and condemned Jesus.

Jesus carried his cross to the hill where he was crucified next to two other criminals, one on his right, the other on his left. Before he died Jesus said, "Father, forgive them, they know not what they do."   *adapted from Luke 23:1–25,33–43*

Forgive as Jesus Did

Sometimes words can become so familiar to us that we don't think about what we are saying. In the Lord's Prayer, look again at the words "forgive us our trespasses, as we forgive those who trespass against us." Now that you have read the story of the Crucifixion, think about what these words mean to you.

Celebrating Lent and Holy Week

The Lenten season is our opportunity to follow Jesus' example in our lives to prepare for Easter. We rededicate ourselves to resist temptation, practice almsgiving, and abstain from meat on Fridays. Making a promise to God and yourself to do something positive or giving toward others is also encouraged.

Write two ways you can celebrate the Lenten season. Choose things that would remind you, daily, of Christ's strength when tempted and his ultimate sacrifice.

_____

_____